A Photo Gallery

Commercial Ships on the
GREAT LAKES

Franz A. VonRiedel

Iconografix

Iconografix
PO Box 446
Hudson, Wisconsin 54016 USA

Library of Congress Control Number: 2005927326

ISBN-13: 978-1-58388-153-8
ISBN-10: 1-58388-153-0

05 06 07 08 09 10 6 5 4 3 2 1

Printed in China

Cover and book design by Dan Perry

Copyedited by Jane Mausser

Cover Photo: Three generations of steamships can be noted in this image taken at the Superior LaFarge Cement terminal. The 1904-vintage *J. B. Ford* is along side the dock, providing additional storage capacity. The WWII-era *Alpena* is off-loading her cargo of cement into the holds of the *Ford*. Both cement carriers were originally constructed as ore boats. Out in the channel, the Str. *Reserve* is on its way to the Allouez ore docks. Built in 1953, this ore carrier is one of many sisters still in operation today. The early 1950s were good years for shipbuilding on the Great Lakes, with many steam turbine powered freighters constructed and most are still in operation today.

Book Proposals

Iconografix is a publishing company specializing in books for transportation enthusiasts. We publish in a number of different areas, including Automobiles, Auto Racing, Buses, Construction Equipment, Emergency Equipment, Farming Equipment, Railroads & Trucks. The Iconografix imprint is constantly growing and expanding into new subject areas.

Authors, editors, and knowledgeable enthusiasts in the field of transportation history are invited to contact the Editorial Department at Iconografix, Inc., PO Box 446, Hudson, WI 54016.

TABLE OF CONTENTS

ACKNOWLEDGEMENTS

Al Hart, Cleveland, OH, photography

Richard Jenkins, Boston, MA, Northeastern Maritime Historical Foundation, research

Jason LaDue, Rochester, NY, photography and research

Jon LaFontaine, St. Paul, MN, LaFontaine - Breda Agency, photography

Roger LeLievre, Ann Arbor, MI, *Know Your Ships*, vessel research

William Moran, Toronto, ONT, *Moran's Shoreside Companion 1997*, vessel research

Capt. Wade Streeter, Detroit, MI, Ferriss Marine Contracting, vessel research

ABOUT THE AUTHOR

Capt. Franz VonRiedel has spent his life persistently documenting the complex histories of the commercial vessels in the maritime industry. He has one of the most comprehensive databases in the country, detailing the history of nearly all the towing vessels and fish tugs in the United States.

Upon graduation from High School, Franz accepted a position as brakeman on an iron ore railroad and after a quick promotion, spent five years working as conductor. From 1997 – 2000, Franz restored and operated the *Marine Trader*, the last commercial bumboat in North America. His company, VonRiedel Marine Services, in addition to scrap and salvage jobs, has handled the brokerage of many vessels on the Lakes and East Coast.

In 2001, Franz expanded his operations to include marine towing. He formed the Zenith Tugboat Company, a namesake that paid tribute to Duluth's historic Zenith Dredge Company and the city's original title of "Zenith City." Today, Zenith Tug owns and operates five towing vessels.

Recognizing his true zeal for marine history, Franz founded the Northeastern Maritime Historical Foundation in 2002, which has become one of the prime contributors to the preservation of the towing industry, in its history and the vessels themselves. The Foundation is dedicated to preserving ships and smaller working vessels that have contributed to the maritime world in significant ways.

Besides his time-consuming business interests and hobbies centered around the maritime industry, he is an avid industrial photographer and has had hundreds of images published throughout the United States and Europe. He also has an immense passion for music played on the Hammond Organ, particularly blues and jazz.

—INTRODUCTION—

For centuries, millions of tons of cargo have moved across the five Great Lakes. The products and commodities from industries of the Midwestern states and Canadian provinces are easily accessible to the world using the St. Lawrence Seaway to reach Lakes Ontario, Erie, Huron, Michigan, and Superior and their contributing waterways.

The Great Lakes region has been constantly on the move beginning in the days when the voyageur's big canoes held payloads easily measured in pounds, to the age of sail when wooden schooners moved between growing ports, to the days of the big steel steamships. Today's modern steel cargo vessels are

capable of taking on more than 60,000 tons in one load. Thanks to far-reaching advances in technology, cargo movement by boat around the lakes became one of *the* safest methods, and provided competitive rates for shipping cargo. It is hard to beat the volume of cargo a Lake freighter can handle in one load.

Cargo still moves, in record numbers, across our clean, cold, freshwater inland lakes, and likely always will. Iron ore mines supply taconite pellets by rail to the ports of Duluth, Allouez, Two Harbors, Silver Bay, and Marquette. Large freighters move the product to the steel mills of Indiana Harbor, Burns Harbor, Gary, Detroit,

Toledo, Lorain, Cleveland, Ashtabula, Conneaut, Nanticoke, and Hamilton.

For decades, a uniquely designed style of freighter has hauled iron ore, either in natural or pellet form. These ships have become known as "ore boats," a designation commonly used by novices to refer to just about any ship on the Lakes.

Tourists and other visitors frequently gather around the canals where these ships enter port. Watching a large inbound vessel gently and quietly glide through the water is quite an experience and can draw a good-sized crowd. People on the pier, especially children, seem mesmerized by the muffled thumping of the engine, the giant propeller churning up the water, and clanging hatch covers on deck as the crews prepare her for loading. Then the deep blast of the steam horns as the captain blows a salute to his fans gazing admiringly from ashore. People wave to the crewmembers on deck, who usually wave back. These sailors have been away from their homes and families for weeks or even months, working long, hard days in weather conditions that most of us cannot even imagine. This life takes a special breed; they generally either love it or hate it.

The Great Lakes have always been known for their unique commercial operations. They are not a place for Z-drive tractor tugs, supertankers, or specialized docking pilots for every ship entering port. The Lakes have always held on to the old-school uses of single screw tugboats, steam propulsion, and incredibly talented engineers and captains who can maneuver their vessels in and out of tight quarters and winding rivers. These Lakes, particularly Lake Superior, can build tremendous seas, rougher than any ocean, and are filled with treacherous shoals, islands, and weather patterns that can change within minutes. They have taken hundreds of freighters and the men who sailed them to their graves.

The Great Lakes are cold. Each year the Lakes and their rivers fill up with ice, either in broken chunks or solid layers, usually several feet thick. Often, as the Coast Guard cutters and privately hired ice breaking tugs break the ice to keep the channels clear, the large chunks of broken ice slide underneath each other, and make the ice twice as thick. In some cases, the rivers fill entirely of ice, which makes navigation impossible.

Shipping operations on the Great Lakes are a seasonal affair. Due to extremely harsh winter weather conditions, ships are forced into winter lay-up that extends from January through March. The lay-ups give crews time to perform the necessary repairs to the vessels, dock facilities, locks, and all the supporting machinery.

While the maritime industry is experiencing great changes in operations, it is undoubtedly at the end of an era. This transition, as with most areas of human interest, brings out the romance and interest in history, of which the Great Lakes are rich in. As the old ways slowly fade, people realize that what they took for granted is changing or disappearing entirely.

The railway caboose is a good example. Many of us remember the days of the mixed freights and waving at the conductor up in the cupola of the brightly colored caboose at the rear of a passing train. Now, those days have ended and an electronic monitoring device has replaced the caboose and the crews who manned them. Nostalgia kicks in and, suddenly, cabooses are in various parks, on display in museums, in a range of artwork, and on children's T-shirts. The entire maritime industry is now in a similar state.

The shipping industry and its colorful past, once in your blood, are hard to ignore. The salt-water industry is also nearing the end of an era. The new tugs are all twin-screw or various styles of "Z-drives." The steamboats are long gone. New security measures restrict access to the port docks and navigable waterways during transit of certain vessels. Even shore-side spectators with cameras are often questioned and many areas have restricted access for shipping enthusiasts. The Lakes are also seeing their share of changes, but, even so, we are lucky enough to still have the privilege of seeing wooden fish tugs, old riveted steel hulls, steam-powered freighters, ancient loading and unloading facilities, and dozens of tugs dating back nearly a century. All of this equipment is professionally maintained and working strong, much like the day it was built.

Although the steamship fleets of the Great Lakes are fairly well documented, there are many other commercial vessels in daily operation that play vital roles in the smooth operations of ports and their visiting ships. This book will review all aspects of commercial vessels currently operating on the Great Lakes, from tugboats to dredges and excursion boats to bumboats. With the declining fleet of old steamships in service, it's often these little guys, the 100-year old tugboats and supply boats, which carry the most history.

Chapter 1: THE LAKER

The "Ore Boat" is just one type of a class of ships, more appropriately referred to as a "Laker," designed for service on the Great Lakes. These Lakers, in all their varieties, haul cargos across all five Lakes, Georgian Bay, the St. Lawrence Seaway to the Atlantic Ocean, down the Erie Canal, and up the navigable rivers that feed ports including Cleveland, on the Cuyahoga River and Chicago, on the Calumet River.

Unlimited fresh water has given an otherwise vulnerable fleet of steamships the ability to last decades longer than its ocean-going counterparts. Lake water is used for cooling the engines and machinery onboard each vessel. As one can imagine, the fresh water of the Lakes is much friendlier on the pipes and heat exchangers than the corrosive salt water of the oceans. Ballast is drawn in from the waters on which the vessel is sailing. Saltwater in a boat's ballast tanks also greatly reduces its life. Even Lakers that occasionally haul salt are found, over time, to have greater corrosion of their cargo holds than those removed from the salt trade.

While ocean-going freighters are built to last 20 to 25 years, it is not uncommon to see a Laker oper-

ating for considerably more than 50 years. Up until the 1980s, many steamers dating back to the 1800s and early 1900s were still in commercial service.

On December 13, 2002, a Friday, an era of the U.S. "straight deckers" ended with the outbound passage of the steamer *Kinsman Independent* from Duluth. "Straight decker" refers to those vessels with long open decks without onboard unloading machinery. Hundreds of these classic steam powered straight-deck bulk carriers once plied the lakes and the *Independent* was the last one in operation.

Since the development of the Lakeboat in the late 1800s, shipbuilders have raced to build them bigger, stronger, and more efficient. In the 1970s, a 1,000-foot vessel was designed and built. These ships remain the maximum size vessel for practical use on the Lakes and are referred to as "Footers." The Footers are too big to transit the St. Lawrence Seaway, the major link from the Great Lakes to the rest of the world, so they are essentially locked in and limited in their trades. It will be interesting to see what the ship of choice on the Lakes will be in another 20 years. Since the Footers built in the 1970s were not as solidly constructed as their pre-WWII counterparts, they have a decreased life expectancy. Because of these factors (but despite the fact that they can carry massive amounts of cargo) many people believe they were an unsuccessful design and that the Lakes will never again see a new Footer built.

After the opening of the St. Lawrence Seaway, many Canadian Lakers were built to the maximum size that could transit the Seaway. This made them rather large capacity ships, versatile because of their Seaway and ocean potential. Built at 730 x 75 feet, these "Seaway carriers," built in the 1960s, make up the bulk of the Canadian fleets today.

On the U.S. side, Seaway length was not as great a concern and in the 1970s, most of the 1950s vintage straight deckers were lengthened by more than 100 feet. The common length of the U.S. ships today is between 750 and 810 feet. Most of the steamboats saw an overhaul in the 1970s that converted the ships to self-unloaders and added length to the vessels, which greatly increased their cargo capacity and versatility. To lengthen a ship, the vessel is placed in dry dock and cut in half. The two halves are spread apart and a new section of cargo hold is built into the middle. Fraser Shipyards in Superior undertook

Awaiting the rest of her load, the steamer *Arthur M. Anderson* is nestled in on the north side of the Duluth Missabi & Iron Range Railway (DM&IR) No. 2 ore dock in Two Harbors. On this warm December night, she, and two other fleet-mates, which will arrive within six hours, will make for a busy night of loading in this small town. Ice is starting to build up on her bow from the freezing spray during the crossing of Lake Superior. The *Anderson* is the ship that was following the *Edmund Fitzgerald* on that fateful night when the *Fitzgerald* was lost in Lake Superior during a November gale.

many of these rebuilds. New midship sections were built in a small graving dock and then floated on their own. Once the new section was ready, the ship was brought into dry dock and cut in half. The new section was floated in and the ship was reassembled. This process greatly reduced downtime for the ship and its owners.

Converting a vessel to a self-unloader, from a straight decker, is another costly process that will take the ship out of service for many months. The vessel's cargo holds have to be reformed into a "V" configuration so that the cargo can slide down the sloping holds into a conveyor system that feeds the unloader boom. When the boom is in position for unloading, gates are opened and the cargo spills slowly onto the belting that takes it down the length of the vessel and up onto the boom, where it is then discharged on shore into hoppers.

Today, almost every ship on the Great Lakes has self-unloading equipment and has been "stretched" to its maximum length. Long and narrow, like a pencil, these Lakeboats have to be carefully designed so that they are not *too* long, which makes them weak in heavy seas. These days, captains and crew are usually very cautious and will go to anchor if the forecast looks bleak. The Lakes have seen their share of shipwrecks through the years and although it has been many years since a major wreck, the possibility is always there. Better safe than sorry.

Since the turn of the century, when wooden schooners were on their way out and new steel freighters were the future, steam has been the power of choice. The triple expansion engine was the most common form of propulsion in Great Lakes freighters. Only a few remain in fleets that once saw hundreds of these engines. Hundreds more still exist at the bottom of the Lakes, still in the vessels for which they were built. (It is truly amazing to imagine what the lakes would look like, if drained for a day. So many famous shipwrecks, such as the *Edmund Fitgerald*, are still there, just out of reach.) Steam propulsion is still prevalent on the Lakes. The turbine engine is the propulsion of choice, or *was*, in the 1950s when the ships were being built. Most ships have two turbines, usually rated at 3,500 to 5,000 SHP each. General Electric, Westinghouse, and DeLaval were the largest makers of steam turbines for Lakeboats.

Diesel ships are typically found with pairs of large Electro Motive or Fairbanks Morse diesel engines. Modern ships, such as the Footers, have variable pitch propellers. These special props allow the blades to turn, on the hub, and change resistance in the water.

The engines do not need to be reversed to change direction. Instead, the propeller blades slowly rotate to a neutral position, so they are just slicing through the water but not moving any water. The blades continue in their rotation until they create an effect that is opposite of forward propulsion and move the ship in reverse. Simply rotating the blades on the propellers changes the speed and direction of the vessel.

Fascinating technology in the mechanical and electrical systems has advanced the Lakers in the past two decades. While the old wooden schooners, straight deck iron freighters, and coal smoke on the horizon are all but gone, the ships that remain all have incredible stories to tell.

After backing out of her berth at Two Harbors, the steamer *A. H. Ferbert* throttles up for departure into Lake Superior downbound for the Soo Locks, indicating her departure with the unmistakable smoke of a steamboat. Having loaded at the ore docks of the DM&IR Railway, this ship is filled with a cargo of iron ore from the Iron Range of Minnesota. Built in 1942, this U.S. Steel "Super" class bulk freighter was named for Adolph Henry Ferbert, who was made president of U.S. Steel's Pittsburgh Steamship Company in 1940. The only one of the Supers to have her first name abbreviated, speculation is that the owners did not want *Adolph H.* on the bow of a ship during WWII. These classic 600-foot U.S. Steel vessels began to lay up in the 1970s as the newer 1,000-foot vessels were built and they finally started going for scrap in the 1980s when a depression in the steel industry had even the new super-carriers temporarily laid up. In 1987, the *Ferbert* was sold to a Turkish scrap yard and was towed overseas the following year. *Photo courtesy of the Northeastern Maritime Historical Foundation*

In Duluth, September 1999, the steamer *Armco*, spins herself around in the East Gate Basin off the Port Terminal. Turning her prop through a reduction gear is a pair of Westinghouse 3,800-HP steam turbines. This vessel, built by the American Shipbuilding Company at Lorain, Ohio in 1953, received its share of modifications through the years, as most do. Staying abreast with the latest technology keeps these Lakers operating efficiently. Bay Shipbuilding of Sturgeon Bay reconstructed the *Armco* with a self-unloading system late in 1981.

The *Algorail*, built in 1968 by Collingwood Shipyards in Collingwood, Ontario, discharges road salt into a rapidly growing pile in Duluth. These self-unloading vessels are versatile, having the ability to swing their own unloading booms out 90 degrees and transfer the cargo by conveyor belt into specific areas or into tight quarters such as hoppers or inside dry storage buildings.

The old coal fired steamer *Joseph Block* sails proudly up the river for another load. Built in 1907 at West Bay City, Michigan, this 556-foot bulk carrier was powered by a triple expansion engine with cylinder diameters of 24, 39, and 65 inches and a stroke of 42 inches, producing 1,850 IHP. On May 22, 1968, the vessel sustained severe damage to her entire bottom after a grounding off Green Bay. Later sold by the underwriters, the former Inland Steel ship was repaired by American Shipbuilding and placed back in service as the *George M. Steinbrenner* the following year. She operated for Kinsman only seven years before laying up and in 1979 was sold to Dwor Metals and dismantled at Ramey's Bend. *Photo courtesy of the Northeastern Maritime Historical Foundation*

The 620-foot Maritimer *George A. Sloan* makes her way slowly through broken, heavy ice just outside Two Harbors on her way to load at the DM&IR ore dock. It is April 24, 1996 and in less than two days she will be fully loaded and downbound on Lake Superior for the Soo Locks but in distress, having suffered mechanical failures. During WWII, 16 nearly identical ships were constructed for various steamship companies on the Lakes. The U.S. Maritime Commission ordered them to increase the iron ore tonnage carried for the war effort. The *Sloan,* being one such vessel, received major modifications including conversion to a self-unloader in 1966. In addition, this modification was needed to fit her in as a replacement for the steamer *Cedarville,* which sank on May 7, 1965. Fraser Shipyards repowered the *Sloan* to diesel in 1985. In 1943, while nearly new, the vessel suffered deck cracking, similar to sister ship *Robert C. Stanley.* This common weakness led to the addition of steel belting, called strapping, to the sides of all Maritimers.

In a very unusual procedure, on April 26, 1996, the disabled *Sloan* was rescued and towed across Lake Superior by one of her fleetmates, the large motor vessel *Roger Blough*. The pair hugged the North Shore to avoid heavy ice flows that had formed in the shipping lanes. Outside Duluth, they were met by the G-Tugs *Kansas* and *North Carolina*, which took the vessel away from the *Blough*. The *Sloan* was towed to the Duluth Port Authority dock where repairs were made, while the *Blough* turned around and made her way back down the Lake for the Soo. The pair was captured on April 27, 1996 in this well-known photograph off Brighton Beach, near Duluth.

Built at Chicago in 1903, the Sand Carrier *Lakewood* is photographed at Cleveland in 1982. When built, this 390-foot vessel was considered large for a bulk freighter. After a long career with the Erie Sand Steamship Company, the vessel was last operated by the Gaelic Tugboat Company of Detroit and finally sold for scrap in 1995. The diesel engine was removed for reuse in a tugboat and the hull was dismantled at Port Maitland. *Al Hart photo*

Upper Lakes Shipping's steamer *Canadian Voyager* heads outbound the Duluth ship canal to clean her holds for the last time. The date is December 10, 2001 and this will be her last trip under her own power. She laid up in Montreal later that month and the following year was sold to Turkish interests for scrap. Originally owned by Canada Steamship under the name *Black Bay*, this Seaway size carrier was powered by 9,000-HP General Electric steam turbines. After a 34-day voyage under tow from Montreal, the *Voyager* was beached at the scrapping facilities of Aliaga, Turkey, exactly 40 years, to the day, since her launching.

The 1908-built *Harvey H. Brown* powers up past Mission Point in the St. Mary's River, downbound. Down below her big funnel, which is belching coal smoke, a triple expansion steam engine is thumping away. With cylinder diameters of 24, 38, and 65 inches and a stroke of 42 inches, this engine produced nearly 1,900 HP and was operated on steam generated by two Scotch boilers. After a long successful career on the Lakes, the poor old steamer sank in the Atlantic Ocean in deep water, about 150 miles off Virginia Beach. The vessel was en route to Mexico to be cut up for scrap. *Photo courtesy of the Northeastern Maritime Historical Foundation*

It would likely be a unanimous vote among enthusiasts on the Lakes that the *Edward L. Ryerson* takes the trophy for prettiest vessel ever built. Built in a unique art-deco style, the 730-foot steamer was constructed by the Manitowoc Shipbuilding Company in 1960. She made history with many "firsts" and a few "lasts" in design and construction. The 9,900-HP vessel made friends all across the Lakes not only for looks but also for her on-board comforts, such as being the first vessel fitted with air-conditioning throughout. The *Ryerson* was also a joy to load, if there is such a thing. She has extra wide hatches and while loading at the gravity dock, does not require as much shifting. She made many record loadings at the port of Two Harbors, with the cooperation of a fast and adept ore dock crew working the chutes. The *Ryerson* laid up in the mid-1990s at Sturgeon Bay, where she is pictured here, with an unknown future. She was the last steamer and last straight-decker built on the U.S. side of the Lakes.

The 580-foot steamer *Henry Phipps* shows us a good example of the standard straight deck ore boat cargo holds. Bulkheads divide the cargo section of each ship's hull into five or six cargo holds. In this photo, chutes from an ore dock are in their lowered position and the cargo is being released from the bins into the ships hold. In this case, the product is a fine-cut natural iron ore, often referred to as "fines" or "mud." Its consistency when exposed to heavy rain turns into just that: mud.

American Shipbuilding built the 680-foot diesel self-unloader *Roger M. Kyes* in 1973 for the American Steamship Company. She was renamed *Adam E. Cornelius* in 1989. She was the fourth vessel to carry that name; the third *Cornelius* is now sailing as the barge *Sarah Spencer*. The fourth *Cornelius* went into service in the ore trade and in the mid 1990s was chartered to Inland Steel after the *Edward L. Ryerson* was laid up in 1994. She is pictured here painted in their colors at the Two Harbors Shiploader (south side of # 2 DM&IR ore dock). Her boom is swinging out to make room for the # 18 and 19 shuttles, topping off her load of taconite pellets from the Minorca mine. In 1999, the vessel was returned to American Steamship and restored to their colors.

This machine is known as a Hullet Unloader. These monstrous steel beasts reached down into the ship's cargo hold, took a bite out of the pile of iron ore, and then pulled back to the dock where it would dump. When the pile got low, bulldozers were lowered into the cargo holds to push smaller piles together to make a large pile that the Hullet could grab. Finally, the deck crews went in with shovels and brooms until every bit was removed. The Hullet unloading process could take days; today's self-unloading vessels can discharge a cargo three times the size in a matter of hours. Notice the man operating the mechanical dinosaur from inside! The date is May 1968 and the ship is the *Benjamin Fairless* unloading at the Gary, Indiana, mill. The *Fairless* was the last of the Super-class to operate as an ore boat. *Author's collection*

11

One of the classic Maritime-class bulk carriers of 1943, *Richard Reiss* is a silhouette against the setting sun in her homeport of Erie. Converted to a self-unloader in 1964 and then converted to diesel in 1976, her triple expansion steam engine was replaced with a single 20-cylinder EMD 645-E6 diesel, which produced 3,000 HP. After a brief lay-up, *Reiss* reentered service in 2004 under the ownership of Grand River Navigation, a company known as one of the primary owners of the remaining classic Lakeboats. This vessel was purchased from the Oglebay Norton Company, which had acquired it through its buy-out of Erie Sand & Steamship. Her self-unloading boom collapsed in the mid-1990s and was removed. Her current boom came off the Canadian Laker *Hochelaga*, which was scrapped at about the same time.

The Canadian shipbuilding companies were still producing beautiful straight deck cargo ships into the 1960s. The *Algocen* was one of the last, built in 1968 by Collingwood Shipyards. A typical "Seaway Carrier," she measures in at 730 feet long by 75 feet wide, about the largest vessel that will fit through the locks of the St. Lawrence Seaway. This size became common for vessels built after completion of the Seaway. She is spotted here on August 11, 2002, taking on cargo at the Agricore United elevator A in Thunder Bay.

Interlake's 1950s steamers *John Sherwin* and *Elton Hoyt 2nd* are shown mothballed in Superior in this December 2001 photo. Because the *Sherwin* is the larger of the two and in better overall condition, a decision was made to sell the *Hoyt* in April of 2003. She was placed into dry dock for inspection at Fraser Shipyards, which is just behind the ships in this photo.

Inspection passed and sale finalized, the vessel was quickly given a high-pressure water blast to knock off all the loose paint and dirt before it could be repainted. Her old Pickands & Mather logo shows through once again after all these years.

The *Hoyt's* anchors and chain were pulled out of the vessel during a thorough inspection. After her water blast, the hull was primered from the keel to the main deck and given a fresh coat of paint in the new owner's color scheme.

The former *Hoyt* is looking sharp as the paint scheme is being completed the night before the tow. It is May 1, 2003 and a tugboat has already arrived to tow the vessel to Sarnia, where her new Canadian owners will complete fit-out. Because of time constraints, the entire process in Superior took place in less than a month.

May 2, 2003, and Gaelic's big lake tug *Roger Stahl* has a hold on the former *Hoyt*, which will soon be renamed *Michipicoten*. They are heading down the front channel in Duluth, about to make the turn for the piers and into Lake Superior on a nice calm evening. They are saluted by the passing *Canadian Olympic* that is arriving to load coal. At the stern of the dead-ship is a G-tug that will assist them out the ship canal.

A couple of months later, the *Michipicoten* overtakes us in Whitefish Bay. She is downbound for Algoma Steel at Sault Ste. Marie, Ontario, loaded with ore from Marquette. Looking sharp in her new color scheme, she leaves a nice wake, steaming proudly down the river.

A frigid December afternoon at the Duluth ship canal never stops a few dedicated visitors from watching a ship pass through. The *Canadian Enterprise* is a modern ship on the Great Lakes, having been built in 1979 in correspondence with the maximum Seaway dimensions. The vessel is powered by twin 4,400-HP Maschinenfabrik Augsburg Nurnberg (known as "MAN") diesels.

In the early morning hours of July 12, 2001, the 730-foot *Canadian Olympic* became entangled with its stern anchor in the Duluth inner anchorage. Caught in the propeller, the anchor chain was later cut off, leaving her anchor on the bottom, while three tugs from the Great Lakes Towing Company towed the disabled vessel into Fraser Shipyards for repair. After two weeks in dry dock, she went back into service.

Under construction at Lorain, in the yards of the American Shipbuilding Company, is what was to be the largest ship on the Great Lakes, the M/V *Roger M. Blough*. One year after this photo was taken, while still under construction, a fire started in her engine room, causing severe damage to that section of the vessel and killing several shipyard workers. After four years of construction, the vessel was finally put into service in 1972, but by that time, the "largest ship on the Lakes" was the M/V *Stewart J. Cort*, which measured 1,000 feet. The *Blough* is 858 feet overall and 105 feet wide, the same width as the 1,000-footers.

When designed, it was thought that she would be the largest vessel that could make the turn around Johnson's Point in the St. Mary's River. The unique stern of the *Roger Blough* shows the doors for the relatively short unloading booms that will extend out 50 feet for off-loading into hoppers. This system limits her to unloading at ports that have the appropriate hopper/conveyor system such as Gary and Conneaut. Her fleetmate *Edgar B. Speer* has similar equipment. She is moored at the Duluth Port Authority dock for winter lay-up in this January 2003 photo.

The *Roger Blough* slides into her berth at the North side of Dock 2 in Two Harbors on a warm summer morning in 1997. The 14,000-HP *Blough* has variable pitch propellers, which allow the vessel to change direction without reversing the engines. During the 1980s, she sat idle, mothballed in Duluth waiting for the domestic steel industry to pick up. By 1987, she was back in action. The *Blough* is truly the last of the "straight deckers" with the forward cabins. Her powerful horns and graceful lines are easy on the eyes for anyone with an appreciation for the beauty in iron.

Built in 1970, the *Stewart J. Cort* was the first 1,000-foot vessel on the Lakes, hence the "#1" painted on her aft cabins. Like the *Roger Blough*, the *Cort* has cabins fore and aft and is also equipped with a small stern mounted retractable self-unloading boom, which limits her discharge capabilities to only a couple of ports. Built for Bethlehem Steel, she has been on the same route her entire life, hauling taconite from the Allouez ore dock of the Burlington Northern Railway to the steel mill at Burns Harbor. In this April 2003 image, she is having difficulties with heavy ice flows that have blown in on western Lake Superior. Her fleetmate *Burns Harbor* waits in the distance, as the *Cort* makes an attempt to back out of the Superior entry through a track that the U.S. Coast Guard Cutter *Sundew* had cut just minutes before.

The 1,000-footer *Columbia Star* was built at Bay Shipbuilding in 1980, completed over the winter, and christened on May 8, 1981. This 14,000-HP vessel is powered by a 4-pack of EMD diesels. All 1,000-foot vessels trade on Lake Superior, taking on cargos of ore and coal from the Twin Ports and North Shore ore loading facilities. The *Star* was the last American-built powered Laker. She is pictured here heading downbound Lake Superior with a load of coal.

The cement carrier *S. T. Crapo* rests at Nicholson's Terminal in Detroit on February 8, 1991. She is holding a winter storage cargo of powdered cement. Silhouetted against a setting sun, her tall stack is classic of the Great Lakes steamship. The wall of steel to her stern, amazingly enough, is another vessel. Dwarfed in comparison to a 1,000-foot carrier, the 402-foot *Crapo* is one of a few small older vessels that have survived in specialized trades. Built much tougher because of the extreme weight of their cargos, the cement carriers were never very long. When she slid down the ways at her 1927 launch, one of her boilers was lit and steam was up, in order to blow a salute on her whistle. *Crapo* was the last coal-fired freighter in operation on the Lakes, when her three original fire tube boilers were converted to burn oil in 1994–95. Less than two years later, the *Crapo* and 1898 fleetmate *E. M. Ford* were replaced by the newly constructed barge, *Integrity*. Both were laid up in September 1996, never to sail again. At that time, the *Crapo* was the last Great Lakes vessel in service powered by a triple expansion steam engine. It ended an era that began with the steamer *Onoko* in 1882.

The *Wolf River* is a 349-foot freighter built as a general freight boat to run the canal system of the St. Lawrence River and Welland Canal. Launched in 1956 as the *Tecumseh*, she has operated under several names and owners over the years. In 1967, the vessel broke in half and sank off Nova Scotia. She was later raised and repaired. Given her present name in 1995, the vessel operated only briefly during 1998, hauling pulpwood from Thunder Bay to Superior. Pulpwood movements were once a common sight on the Lakes. We passed the loaded vessel in this June 30, 1998 photo, as she crossed Lake Superior bound for the Duluth entry. After only a few trips this year, the vessel went into lay-up, where she remains today.

Built by the famous Alexander McDougall in Duluth, the *Day Peckinpaugh* began life as a general cargo ship for the New York State Barge Canal system. Five identical vessels were built for the Interwaterway Lines in 1921, and given a generic series of names; this one was called *I. L. I. 101*. Long, slender, and extremely low, these freighters could pass under the rather low bridges of the Erie Canal and run the entire length from Tonawanda to Waterford. A pair of Detroit 6-110 Diesels (producing only 440 HP) powers this 260-foot freighter. Many people think she is the last of her kind, but the *I. L. I. 105* also remains, abandoned along the banks of Staten Island in the famed Witte's boneyard.

The steamer *Kinsman Independent* was the second vessel to wear that name and she wouldn't be the last. She worked for Kinsman only nine years before being sold for scrap and towed to Turkey in the Summer of 1988, in a tandem tow with the first *Oakglen*, a nearly identical sister ship. The American Shipbuilding Company built both ships in 1923. In 1989, the *Independent* was dismantled on the beaches of Aliaga. The classic straight decker is pictured in Cleveland with a grain load on July 27, 1984. *Al Hart photo*

The 640-foot *Kinsman Independent* (the third) has only two years left in her career at the time of this November 2000 photo. She is taking on a cargo of grain at Harvest States No. 1 in Superior, bound for the elevators of Buffalo. She would make the same voyage in December of 2002 and then lay up in Buffalo, where she was scavenged until finally being sold Canadian. The once proud bulk carrier began life as the *Charles L. Hutchinson* and was later renamed *Ernest R. Breech* for the Ford Motor Company. Her steam turbine engines were built by the Bethlehem Steel Company for the *Aloca Prospector*, which was torpedoed and sunk during WWII and later salvaged. Upon her lay-up, she ended the era of U.S. flag straight-deck carriers on the Lakes.

Calcite II is getting ready to load at the DM&IR ore dock in Duluth on June 14, 1997. Built as a steamer, her triple expansion engine was replaced in 1964 with a Nordberg diesel. The steam venting near her bow is evident her boiler is still in use; steam is generated to operate machinery such as winches and the ship's heating system. In this image, she is wearing fresh paint from bow to stern. The ship was converted to a self-unloader in 1961 to replace the *Carl D. Bradley*, which foundered in a Lake Michigan gale on November 18, 1958.

Upper Lakes Shipping's *Canadian Ranger* has an unmistakable profile from any angle. Unique to the *Ranger*, she has her entire superstructure aft, but her self-unloading rigging and boom are in the bow. This ship was reconstructed in 1983 by combining the best of two ships: the stern section and engine room from the 1967 *Canadian Chimo* and the bow and cargo section from the 1961 German *Hilda Marjanne*. In this photo, the joint between the two is obvious and shows the additional width of the bow and cargo section. Five years after this conversion, the unique self-unloading system was added.

The Imperial Oil Company, one of the oldest steamship companies on the Lakes, operated a large fleet of tankers since their beginning in 1899. Like most Imperial fleet tankers, the *Sarnia* has the graceful lines of the early style, with the superstructure amidships and the tall steam stack. Sold to Provmar Terminals in 1986, she was renamed *Provmar Terminal II*, as shown in this January 1998 photo; she sits inactive in Hamilton. This 1948 vintage petroleum tanker is powered by a pair of Inglis Company 1,450-HP steam turbines that were built in Toronto. Measuring 408 feet long, this vessel has 14 cargo tanks and a capacity of 1,925,000 gallons. Since her retirement in 1986, she, like many classic Lakers, has played the roll of a storage hull.

Pictured here is the 640-foot steamer *John J. Boland* during her last season of operation by American Steamship Company. Built in 1953 and designed to haul coal, the *Boland* is one of very few remaining ships that have telescoping hatch covers that open using steam winches, cables, and related rigging. The covers are tightly secured and tarped for the heavy seas during Lake crossings. Most vessels have large single piece hatches that are opened by a hatch crane that runs on rails the length of the deck.

Unfavorable weather has the *John J. Boland* riding out the storm in port. Loaded with coal bound for Taconite Harbor on the North Shore of Lake Superior, a break in the weather is anticipated and the vessel is scheduled to sail again, soon. Near the gangway, a departure time is noted on the board.

The *Saginaw* is outbound Duluth on a cold October afternoon after loading taconite at the Missabe ore docks. At the time of this photo, she has sailed for Lower Lakes almost one year, proudly wearing her new colors. Formerly the *John J. Boland*, this steamer became the fifth vessel in the Lower Lakes/Grand River fleet.

In the spring of 2003, a dam in Marquette crumbled, causing major flooding and damage to the power plant. Power at the mine was reduced to enable the City to continue with electricity. With emergency repairs in progress, June saw the start of a busy summer at the Lake Superior & Ishpeming ore dock. On a run to the Ford Motor Company's plant in Detroit, two Interlake steamers are taking on cargos of ore. On one side, the *Lee A. Tregurtha* is already loading, while the *Kaye E. Barker* slides into the other for the same product. The *Kaye E.* is the only AAA-class vessel built with a triple-deck forward end.

The *Algosound* was the last steam-powered vessel operating for the Algoma Central fleet when sold for scrap in 2003. Originally named *Don-De-Dieu* for the Papachristidis Fleet, this straight-decker was powered by two Canadian GE steam turbines, totaling 9,900 SHP. The *Algosound* was fit-out for service late in 2002 after a brief lay-up but the following year was sold for scrap and towed overseas in the spring of 2004. In 1979, she was temporarily renamed *Edmund Fitzgerald* for a feature film of the historic sinking. While the film was never completed, the footage was later used in a History Channel documentary about the wreck. The vessel you see in that film is actually the Canadian steamer *Algosound*. In this photo, she is loading at Harvest States No. 1 in Superior and Bernard Kaner's bumboat *Kaner I* is tied alongside and open for business. *Jon LaFontaine photo*

Operating today as the *Cedarglen*, this view of Paterson's *Cartierdoc* shows her loading at Harvest States No. 2 in Superior. The hull was originally the *Ems Ore*, built in Hamburg, Germany in 1959. The Jones Act prohibits U.S. vessel owners from operating hulls that are not built in the States. However, once the St. Lawrence Seaway opened in 1959, large freighters were able to fit into the Lakes and since then many Canadian steamship companies have purchased foreign hulls for conversions into lake carriers. The same pilothouse she has today was originally placed amidships.

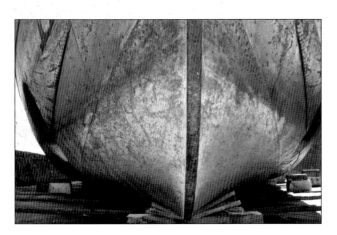

This angle gives this dry-docked hull a small appearance, making it look no different than any other vessel, such as a tug or passenger vessel. Amazingly, it is the bow of the 640-foot self-unloader *Canadian Transfer,* sitting on the blocks for repairs. Her bow thruster tunnel is visible on both sides. Before a vessel is placed into dry dock, the shipyard must obtain a docking plan that shows the entire layout of the underside of the vessel. With this plan, they will know where to set their blocking. Large timber blocks for the ship to rest on are pinned into place. The dry dock is flooded, the ship is towed into place, the gates are closed, the water is then pumped out, and the ship settles gently onto its blocks.

The Laker *Consumers Power* of the Erie Sand Steamship fleet is seen here discharging her aggregate cargo in Cleveland on June 13, 1984. This classic steamboat sank after a collision in 1943 and was raised in a rather ingenious manner by the famous Captain John Roen, who then took ownership of the vessel, even though it was a total loss. He used two large barges, as pontoons, alongside the sunken freighter and raised it slowly through a series of small lifts, while pumping air in and water out. The vessel was repaired and placed back into service for another 42 years before it was towed to Taiwan for scrap. *Al Hart photo*

The *Power* was re-engined in 1956: her original triple expansion engine was replaced with a 5,500-SHP compound turbine. Originally christened *George M. Humphrey*, she was built in 1927 by American Shipbuilding in Lorain as hull number 796. *Al Hart photo*

Docked at the West DM&IR # 6 gravity dock in Duluth, Oglebay Norton's motor vessel *Fred R. White Jr.* is taking a break from loading while ballast water is pumped out. Alongside is the bumboat *Marine Trader*, from which the crew can get their supplies without heading up town. The date is July 10, 1998.

Wintering in Thunder Bay, the *Scott Misener* awaits another season of work in this March 1992 photo. Launched as the *J. N. McWatters* in 1961, she sailed for the Misener fleet until 1994 when Algoma Central bought her. The vessel then sailed as the *Algogulf*, until being sold for scrap in 2002. McKeil Marine towed the vessel to Port Colborne and docked her at the International Marine Salvage yard. After abatement work, the torches cut into her stern in October of 2002 and within the next 16 months, she was completely gone. *Jon LaFontaine photo*

March 1999 finds the *Algosound*, with a storage cargo, alongside Paterson's *Comeaudoc* in winter lay-up in Montreal. The 1965-vintage *Algosound* is the last steam-powered ship in the Algoma Central fleet. Scrapping is inevitable for both of these vessels. Hundreds of classic Canadian steamers have made their way to the scrappers and to this date, not one has been preserved as a museum vessel.

Lay-up is a time for sprucing up the hulls. During any other time of the year they are heavily laden with cargo and sitting low in the water and therefore inaccessible for proper painting. While the cold winter sets in and ice closes in tight around each vessel, shipyard crews drag large sections of scaffolding out and with long sticks and rollers apply fresh paint to the hulls. Even though several inches of water surround the vessel where they are working, the workers can rest assured that a good two feet of ice is below them. In this March photo, workers from Fraser Shipyard carefully paint new stripes and draft marks on the *Cason J. Callaway*, of the USS Great Lakes Fleet. With empty cargo holds and dry ballast tanks, the steamship sits very high in the water, even fully exposing her bow thruster tube (which is an interesting comparison in size to the workers). *Jon LaFontaine photo*

Come spring, fresh paint over winter lay-up leaves three U.S. Steel 600-footers looking sharp. A Manitowoc crane has boomed down pretty far to set a piece of machinery into the gangway door on the *Robert C. Stanley* (built in 1943 by Great Lakes Engineering Works). In her first year of service, the *Stanley's* deck split in two during a storm. Cables were strung between the fore and aft winches in order to hold the ship together until they made port. After that, belting was applied to the sides of all Maritimer-class vessels, which solved the problem. Outboard of her, in this image, is the steamer *Benjamin F. Fairless* (1942) and against the wall is the *Homer D. Williams*, the oldest of the bunch, having been built in 1917 at AmShip's Lorain yard. These are truly "ore boats" at their finest.

The 730-foot *Algowest* sits in the Port Weller Dry Dock on this foggy January morning in 1998. The ship is about to undergo a conversion to a self-unloader. Alongside is fleet-mate *Algorail*; both ships were built by Collingwood Shipyards.

At the end of the 2000 season, U.S. Steel's Great Lakes Fleet sold off three of their smaller self-unloaders. The *George A. Sloan* was sold Canadian to Lower Lakes Towing and the *Calcite II* and *Myron C. Taylor* were sold to Grand River Navigation, LLT's U.S. subsidiary. In this 1998 photo, both the *Taylor* and *Calcite II* lay for winter repairs at Bay Shipbuilding. Both vessels were constructed as steam bulk carriers in 1929 and later repowered with single 3,200-HP Nordberg diesels. They sailed for U.S. Steel's Bradley Fleet, working mostly in the limestone trade and wearing gray hull colors through the 1980s.

The weather looks decent in this March 1999 photo and the owners are likely anxious to get moving, but it's an extended winter lay-up in Montreal, Quebec, one of the largest lay-up ports on the Canadian side. Having arrived Christmas day 1998, the *Enerchem Trader* will not sail again under her Canadian ownership. The company is about to be sold to Algoma Tankers Ltd and the *Trader* is scheduled to be renamed *Algotrader*, a name she will never see. After sitting out of service for another year, the vessel was sold foreign in April 2000 and operated in the Persian Gulf area under a Panamanian flag. Due to corrosion from salt water, the tanker *Edouard Simard* was worn out and ready for scrap less than 20 years after she was built in 1961. In 1978, an entirely new mid-body (cargo section) and bow was constructed and fitted to the old stern (engine room) section. With new piping and a complete overhaul, this old tanker was again essentially a brand new ship. Ironically, only another 20 years later, once again, she was wearing thin and this time faced the inevitable. In January 2003, she was sold for scrap and arrived on the beach at Gadani, Pakistan where she was dismantled.

Winter lay-up at St. Catherines on the Welland Canal is a busy place for ship repairs. Here, a shipyard welder completes a large patch to the side of the motor vessel *Sauniere*. This vessel was built in 1970 as the bulk carrier *Brooknes* at Scotland before being sold to Canadian interests in 1975. At that time, the ship was cut in half, lengthened by 120 feet, and converted to a self-unloader.

In her Sarnia, Ontario, lay-up berth, Algoma Central's self-unloader *Agawa Canyon* waits out the winter on this cold January night in 1998. Sarnia, across from Port Huron on the St. Clair River, is one of the lay-up ports for Canadian ships and is filled with activity in the winter.

The *Halifax* of the Canada Steamship Lines (CSL) fleet unloads into the Cargill B-2 elevator in Duluth. As the last steamer in the CSL fleet, she is powered by a pair of Inglis steam turbines, which produce 10,000 HP. Standard Seaway size, 730 x 75 feet, this 20,646-gross-ton vessel was built in 1963 by Davie Shipbuilding at Lauzon, Quebec, for the Hall Corporation and launched as the *Frankcliffe Hall*. She was given her current name in 1988 when sold to CSL.

Gary, Indiana, "a friendly steel mill town" is the port of call for this Canadian self-unloader *Rt. Hon. Paul J. Martin* on November 23, 2002. She is discharging her cargo of 32,000 tons of iron ore pellets into a small hopper that feeds into a belt system that takes the product to the stockpiles. This vessel underwent an extensive reconstruction in 2000, when her stern (engine room section) was cut off. It was reattached to an entirely new cargo hold and bow section, increasing her tonnage capacity and giving the vessel all new piping, ballast tanks, thruster, and cargo holds. For those who have seen the movie "Pearl Harbor;" towards the end when an attack against a Japanese tank and ammunition plant is executed, take careful note when the planes first fly into this area from the sea. Those poor guys must have taken a wrong turn and bombed Gary, Indiana instead.

Catherine Desgagnes (pronounced "da gon yay") is one of many vessels owned by the Desgagnes Company, which operates a fleet of tankers and bulk carriers on the Canadian side. This particular bulker was built in Aberdeen, Scotland, in 1962 and sold Canadian in 1972. These small 400-foot freighters are versatile in the small ports and shallow waters where they can operate. She is pictured here in Milwaukee in November 1994. *Jon LaFontaine photo*

Winter takes its toll on hulls, with heavy ice flows jamming the commercial waterways of these inland ports. In Duluth, temperatures well below zero and severe winds created an ice field in the harbor that went from open water to ice 16 feet thick in less than a month's time. Here, the footer *Indiana Harbor* is using all of her 14,400 HP yet hardly budging an inch. Tugboats and the Coast Guard icebreaker *Sundew* do what they can to break trail ahead of the vessel, which is loaded with coal and trying to depart the Duluth ship canal. While crossing the frigid waters of Lake Superior, heavy seas send water crashing over the top of the bows, instantly freezing to the ship. Vessels often enter port with bows encrusted with ice several feet thick.

The motor vessel *Ralph Misener* was built with an unusual experimental self-unloader known as the "Conflo Unloading System." The large deck-mounted unit was considered a failure and eventually suffered severe damage in a 1976 storm when it was improperly secured. The following year, Davie Shipbuilding removed it. In 1994, Misener Transportation sold the *Ralph* to Upper Lakes Shipping, which in turn renamed the vessel *Gordon C. Leitch*. Built in 1968 to Seaway size, she is still in service, powered by one 6-cylinder 9,600-HP Sulzer diesel. *Author's collection*

The U.S. Steel self-unloader *John G. Munson* discharges her cargo of limestone into the pile at the Cutler Magner facility in Superior. Many limestone cargos are hauled into the Twin Ports and then taken by rail to the mines of northern Minnesota, where they are used in the process of making taconite pellets. This one-owner vessel has been a part of the U.S. Steel fleet since it was built in 1952 as Hull No. 412 at the Manitowoc Shipbuilding Company. The early 1950s, particularly 1952, were incredible years on the Lakes for shipbuilding, as many turn-of-the-century steamships were retiring and being replaced by larger modern carriers. She is the oldest vessel in operation on the Lakes built as a self-unloader. She claimed that title in 1995, when her fleetmate *Irvin L. Clymer* (1917), was scrapped at Duluth.

Built in 1958 by American Shipbuilding at Toledo, the steam turbine-powered *John Sherwin* was still quite young when she went into lay-up on November 16, 1981 in Superior. The downturn of the steel industry in the 1980s made it no surprise to see her at the wall. A decade passed and the 1990s brought out many rumors. Would she be fit out again, converted to a self-unloader, made into a tug barge unit, or would she be sold for scrap? Rumors came and rumors went, while *Sherwin* sat patiently at Fraser Shipyards. Twenty-five years now and she still sits out, waiting for a change in the industry that would justify the refit of an 806-foot ship that has been sitting idle for more than half of its life. Although since converted to oil, she was the last coal fired ship built on the Lakes when she was built.

Each vessel is unique in its own way, and for some it's appearance. Algoma Central's *Algosoo* is no exception. Her graceful lines were assembled at the Collingwood Shipyard in 1974. At Seaway length, this self-unloader is powered by a pair of Pielstick 10-cylinder diesels, totaling 9,000 HP, standard for a vessel of this size. The *Algosoo* primarily hauls cargos of taconite and coal between U.S. and Canadian ports. She was the last Laker to be built with the pilothouse forward.

Upbound in the Detroit River is the veteran cement carrier *Southdown Challenger*. She is distinct on the lakes in a variety of ways. When built in 1906 she was considered a "lakes leviathan." Now the largest ships sailing the lakes are just under twice the size of the *Challenger*. She holds the distinction of being the oldest operating ship on the lakes. She is the largest cement carrier, and can unload faster than any other cement carrier on the lakes. She also has a rare high-pressure, 4-cylinder Skinner Uniflow Marine Steam Engine, of which only a handful remain in the world. The 552-foot riveted steel vessel was converted to haul cement in 1967. Visible at the forward end is the boom used to offload the cement.

This is a view from the deck of the classic cement carrier *Southdown Challenger* as she unloads at Southdown's Detroit Terminal. Clearly visible are the small scuttle hatches used for loading the dry powder cement. A reciprocating steam winch is also visible in the photo. Most cement boats use air and conveyors to move the cement from the ship to the silo. However, some cement boats still use old screw type pumps to discharge, a system that takes longer than the more modern air/conveyor process.

The first ever purpose-built cement carrier *Lewis G. Harriman* was always a tight squeeze when trying to fit into her berth at the cement silos way up river in Milwaukee. With the help of two or three Selvick tugs from Sturgeon Bay, the ship was carefully maneuvered around 90-degree turns, one after another, until finding home at her owner's elevator. After construction of a new silo in the main harbor, the 1923-vintage steamer was no longer needed and was sold to St. Mary's Cement, which used it in Green Bay for a few years as a storage hull. In 2003, Northeastern Maritime, a museum organization, tried with great effort to save the vessel, but a simple miscommunication between accounting and operations led to the vessel being relinquished for scrap instead. After only a few months, what was an amazing time capsule of Great Lakes history became a rusting hulk sitting in the scrap yard and lacking major collectible components that had managed to stay with the inactive vessel for over two decades. The vessel was always rumored to be a stripped hulk and nothing but a "pigeon coop." To the contrary, the *Harriman* was amazingly well preserved and left fully intact, with portholes and doors sealed tight to project her from unwanted cement dust blowing in. The loss of the *Harriman* was a sad event for many steam preservationists in the United States.

This is the standard galley of a steamship. Food is plentiful on the Lakers and for the most part, known to be very well prepared. One way to keep a crew happy is to keep them fed. This view shows the galley of the steamer *Lewis G. Harriman*, as she sits awaiting the beginning stages of scrapping. Eighty years earlier, the *Harriman* was brand new, and christened at her launching by the daughter of Mr. S. T. Crapo.

Looking down toward the bilge, one of *Harriman's* rods connects to the crankshaft under the cylinders of her huge triple expansion steam engine. This ship was built by the Toledo Shipbuilding Company, which also constructed its own line of engines. The *Harriman*, originally named *John W. Boardman*, had the same engine for her entire career. Only two years before going into permanent lay-up, her boilers were rebuilt and converted to burn oil.

Harriman was in immaculate condition for a vessel that was laid up 23 years before her sale to the scrappers. Pictured is her original tongue and groove woodwork, light fixtures, old-fashioned bunks, portholes with battle covers, sink, and mirror. These are comfortable quarters for this 1920s era ship. This is one of the crew quarters on the main forecastle deck in the bow area. Five minutes with a bottle of cleanser would make it ready for use. Instead, it will soon be gutted for scrapping.

Down in the belly of the beast and well below the waterline, this view shows what it looks like below the cargo holds. Self-unloading vessels have slanted holds, which funnel the cargo down to large gates that can be opened to various degrees, thereby controlling the flow of the cargo onto a conveyor belt system that moves the product into the unloading system. This view shows the double holds that slant down toward two conveyor systems on the cement carrier *Lewis G. Harriman*.

U.S. Steel's *Philip R. Clarke* is breaking a trail through thick ice on Lake Superior early in the navigation season. She has yet to be converted to a self-unloader and is a true straight-decker in this image. Off her port stern, she has passed fisherman's ice-houses about a mile off.

Canada Steamship Lines' *Simcoe* was sold to Algoma Central in 1994 and renamed *Algostream*. Beginning the season in CSL colors with the billboard name painted over, the *Algostream* was soon in full Algoma livery, but would never see service again after laying up at the end of that year. Sold for scrap in 1995, she was towed from the Lakes in October. The tow only made it to Namibia, where she sat over a pay dispute. Finally arriving in Alang, India, in November 1996, the vessel was beached for scrapping, which was completed in 1997.

It is January 1995 and American Steamship's M/V *St. Clair* is moored for winter at Hallett Dock # 5 in West Duluth. Before a special unloading and conveyor system was built into the DM&IR ore dock, limestone was unloaded at Hallett 5. Large front-end loaders filled side dump train cars with the stone, which was then transported north to the mines. Limestone is used in the process of making taconite pellets.

The *Algonorth* is pictured at AGP 6 in Duluth on a late November night in 2002. Built as the 525-foot Scottish bulk carrier *Temple Bar*, she was later lengthened and converted for Great Lakes service. She is able to carry roughly 28,000 tons and can run at a speed of 16 MPH. Her large, upturned, bulbous bow gives her a unique appearance for a Lake-boat.

In a rare move, CSL's *Tadoussac* is seen taking on a cargo from Hallett Dock No. 5 in West Duluth, as dark storm clouds move in. It is common for ships to unload stone at this facility, which is then loaded into train cars and trucks by loaders. In the foreground, loaders have taken bites out of a pile that was once an entire ship's cargo and now, with the majority of it gone, the center remains, forming a unique natural sculpture.

Many of the Lakers wore, at one time, the name of the owners in billboard lettering down the sides of their hulls. This example shows Canada Steamship Lines' motor vessel *Manitoulin*, built at Lauzon, Quebec, in 1966. She was the first self-unloader built by Davie Shipbuilding. At Seaway size, 730 x 75-feet, she was sold for scrap in 2001 and towed overseas.

Loading at the Peavey elevator in Superior, the *Oakglen* enjoys her last year with the Parrish & Heimbecker (P&H) fleet. She would soon be sold to back to Canada Steamship Lines (CSL) and operate only briefly before being sold for overseas scrapping. This beautiful 714-foot Laker was built for CSL in 1954 as the *T. R. McLagan* and was sold in 1990 to P&H Shipping. Powered by twin Westinghouse steam turbines, the 8,500-HP straight deck grain ship was towed to Aliaga, Turkey, and scrapped in 2004. Like many Lakers before her, she was in immaculate condition when sold for scrap, with a spotless engine room, and pilothouse that shone of brass, copper, and stainless steel, with a wooden binnacle and wheel.

The *Fraser* is shown at Fraser Shipyards, May 1990. The 600-foot steamer *Leon Fraser* was retired from the U.S. Steel fleet in 1981 and sold for use as a museum ship in Lorain, Ohio. After a brief ownership, the vessel was resold, again for commercial use. The *Fraser* was towed to Fraser Shipyards in Superior in 1989 and placed in the dry dock. The vessel was cut in half and shortened 120 feet in order to strengthen the hull for cargos of cement, and to allow the vessel to fit into cement terminals in small ports. The vessel was reconstructed, renamed *Alpena*, and re-entered service as a cement carrier in 1991. *Jon LaFontaine photo*

Moored at the Cleveland LaFarge terminal, the classic stern of the *Alpena* shows her obvious origins as a 1940s Laker. It may be a bit premature to predict that the *Alpena* will be the last operating steamer on the Lakes, but she is certainly one of the better maintained.

The cement carrier *J. A. W. Iglehart* is pictured here on August 18, 2001 in Detroit. She began life in 1936 as the Pan American Petroleum tanker *Pan-Amoco*, later sailing as *Amoco*, and finally as *H. R. Schemm*, before she was converted to a cement carrier and given her present name in 1965. She is still powered by her original 4,400-HP DeLaval steam turbines and is a true workhorse for the Inland Lakes Transportation fleet. This makes her the oldest working Laker with her original engine.

Canadian Mariner gets a coat of fresh paint as she loads at AGP in Duluth on June 3, 1995. Built by Saint John Shipbuilding at Saint John, New Brunswick, in 1963, she was originally named *Newbrunswicker*. She is powered by two Canadian GE steam turbines, totaling 9,900 SHP. When new, she was part of the Papachristidis fleet.

At the far western end of Lake Superior, the steamer *Philip R. Clarke* lines up for the canal entrance to Duluth. She will discharge her cargo of limestone at the Missabe ore dock's stone hopper and then head back out empty, stopping in the port of Two Harbors to take on a load of taconite. An ocean-going grain ship is sitting in the anchorage area outside the harbor, awaiting her berth at an elevator.

The *Lee A. Tregurtha* was built in 1941 as a civilian tanker for the Socony Oil Company. Upon completion in 1942, the U.S. Navy requisitioned her for service in WWII. Christened USS *Chiwawa* AO-68, the Auxiliary Oiler entered service on February 13, 1943 and saw her fair share of action around the world over the next several years. Earning two battle stars in the war, she was the class boat for the *Chiwawa*-class T-3 tankers. After decommissioning, the vessel joined a MarAd reserve fleet where she sat until 1961 when Cleveland Cliffs purchased the vessel for conversion into a Laker. Still in service, the *Lee A. Tregurtha* is photographed here upbound waiting to enter the Soo Locks on June 21, 2001. She is the largest steam powered freighter on the Lakes.

Making a late season ore run, crewmembers climb back aboard the steamer *Lee A. Tregurtha* after fueling at the Murphy Oil dock in Duluth. The date is December 28, 1996 and heavy ice is starting to form in the harbor. The tug *North Carolina* is out breaking ice around the ship as she prepares to get underway at dusk. Ice from heavy seas has formed on the entire length of her hull and is especially thick on the bow.

The *Middletown* has just arrived at Silver Bay on a September morning, 2002. Ballast water is being discharged as her crew finishes securing the mooring lines. Built in 1943 for the Maritime Administration as the USS *Neschanic*, this steamer began life as an oil tanker. During WWII, she earned nine battle stars and was involved in nearly every major battle in the Pacific during the war. She was sold into civilian ownership after the War. While working for Gulf Oil in 1958, she collided with the gasoline tanker *S. E. Graham* and burned until she was a total loss with 15 casualties. The vessel was salvaged and three years later, she was converted to a bulk carrier for use on the Great Lakes.

This is the classic tall funnel of the steamboats. Oglebay Norton Company's logo has replaced the *Middletown* Columbia star insignia she wore for more than three decades. If you look closely, the "G" from her Gulf Oil days can still be seen, under many coats of paint. Protruding from her stack are twin Leslie Tyfon DVE-300 steam horns, a standard arrangement on the steamships of the Lakes.

The steamer *Harry Coulby*, measuring in at 631 feet long, could only carry about one quarter of the load taken on by today's modern footers. Nevertheless, the fine craftsmanship of those old steamers could not be beaten. Shining of copper, brass, and systems of old, the Lakers were beautifully made vessels. Here, brass railings surround her large wooden wheel while the gyro repeater and binnacle also shine of brass. To the right, the pilothouse is sporting its beanbag ashtray, a seemingly standard piece of equipment for every pilothouse. Imagine the action that has been seen from these windows throughout her 70-year career.

It's July 1, 1994 and the 1927 vintage steamer *Kinsman Enterprise* is in for repairs, at the AGP Cap. 6 dock in Duluth. A thunderstorm is moving in while the vessel's crew relaxes after a day of work on board. These down times are a good chance to catch up on the needed cleaning and repairs that are difficult to do while underway. A storm doesn't bother this old girl, as she stands tall and proud, with her steering pole extended out, ready to guide the wheelsman on her next voyage across the lake.

Steam on a steamship does not just power the main engine. It also powers the ship's generators, as seen in this photo. Steam is also used to run the deck winches and is piped through registers in all the rooms for heat. A Laker's engine room is a maze of piping, wiring, gauges, switches, valves, levers, pumps, and blowers that takes a crew of very experienced engineers to operate. Without an ace engine crew, the ship does not move. This engine-room pictured is the 1927-built *Kinsman Enterprise*.

A photo that is worth a thousand words can often be so simple. An example is the old riveted hull plating of a steamship where layer upon layer of paint would reveal old paint schemes. All the machinery on board is cooled using water. Fresh water is pulled in and cycled though heat exchangers, much like a radiator in an automobile, but larger. The lake water never touches the dirty parts and pieces, it only "mingles" with the hot water that is trapped in an enclosed system, passing through tubes, doing its part to cool the system, and then it is pumped back over the side, still as clean as it was when pulled in.

Heading out across Lake Superior on her last voyage, the steamer *Kinsman Enterprise* is loaded with grain for Buffalo. On a cold miserable day in typical Lake Superior fog and blizzard conditions, her crew is busy on deck securing hatches in preparation for the worst. Once a common sight on the lakes, these American straight deckers are all now retired. When built, the *Enterprise* was the largest ship on the Lakes. She was the last pre-WWII straight-decker in service when she retired; the fleet had dwindled from literally hundreds down to this one lonesome steamboat.

Chapter 2: TUGBOATS

Tugboats have been on the scene since the beginning of commercial navigation. Performing towing and assistance duties all across the Great Lakes, these powerful workboats are no more than an engine with a pilothouse on it. Tugboats come in all shapes and sizes, from the small 40-foot dredge tending tugs, or "tenders," to the big 150-foot over-lake towing tugs. Some standard designs ply the Lakes, as do many one-of-a-kind towing vessels.

The "cute little harbor tugs," as they are often described, are actually far from little. They are only small when compared to the massive Lakeboats. Harbor tugs are rather large and have systems and engine room layouts resembling large ships. The harbor tugs on the Great Lakes are unique to this region. Most have a low profile design and are useful while working in the tight quarters of the winding rivers found in and around most harbors. Tight turns, close bridges, and the large flared bows of the ocean going ships call for small but powerful tugs that are low enough to duck under all of these obstructions. If a tug is too tall, the upper structure is easily damaged;

traditional harbor tugs frequently have bent visors and handrails.

In the 1890s, owners of the Great Lakes steamship companies put together a tug company consisting of several existing Lakes towing companies in an effort to gain more control over the service and rates for vessel assistance. In 1899, nearly all the independent tug companies were purchased and consolidated, forming the Great Lakes Towing Company.

The acquisition of these companies included a large fleet of medium-sized wooden harbor tugs. After the turn of the century, with the rapid growth in the size and style of cargo ships, these old wooden steam tugs were increasingly outdated and the need was great for a newer, more powerful design. The tug company, commonly referred to as "The Towing Company," began a program to build new tugs, specifically for performing harbor assist duties for large steel freighters unique to the Great Lakes.

Over the course of 20 years, dozens of these large, 81-foot, riveted steel, low profile, steam-powered, ship-docking tugs were constructed by and for the Towing Company. These tugs, because of the trademark "G" logo on their smokestacks, have become known affectionately as "G-tugs." Many received second hand engines salvaged from obsolete old wooden tugs. Others were powered by a standard 25 x 28-inch bore and stroke single-cylinder non-condensing high-pressure steam engine, built by the Towing Company.

In the 1950s, this same fleet of vintage steam tugs was converted from steam to diesel and the profile design was modified to eliminate the main deckhouse. Reconstructed with barely a cabin, other than a pilothouse and small "trunk" above the engine room, these freshly rebuilt tugs were cutting-edge design for ship docking tugs on the Lakes.

While a few tugs received EMD 567 engines or experimental Cleveland 498s, the bulk of the fleet saw Cleveland 12-cylinder, 1200-HP 278A diesels. About half were given gearboxes that included air clutches, while the others had DC electric propulsion motors, rated at about 900 HP. Even today, these diesel tugs make up the majority of the Great Lakes Towing harbor tug fleet.

Other independent tug companies, such as Basic Marine Towing, Calumet River Fleeting,

Ship-docking tugs, unique to the Great Lakes, are the "G-tugs" of the Great Lakes Towing Company. Here, the 1910 vintage *North Dakota* breaks out the Duluth harbor on December 11, 2000. The captain uses the tug's sleek hull to bust through the heavy ice that forms in the harbor and then uses the wake to roll the ice, breaking it slowly as they run back and forth. As this process is repeated again and again, broken ice chunks refreeze, creating layers of solid ice that are commonly several feet thick.

Gaelic Tugboat Company, Selvick Marine Towing, and the Zenith Tugboat Company use a variety of styles. Many tugs have come off the ocean and are traditional, two-deck, harbor tugs. Others are heavily built, traditionally styled Army or Navy tugs purchased at government auctions. A few G-tugs have escaped from the Towing Company through the years and can be found in private fleets. Others began life with big marine contracting outfits that had powerful tugs built to handle lake towing. As the contractors went out of business, many of these boats have made their way into the harbor assist and ice breaking trades.

Harbor tugs are rarely called out on nice calm warm summer days; they are summoned in the worst of weather. When there is a snow squall, the wind is howling, seas are heavy, ice is 14 inches thick, and visibility is zero due to fog, it is *then*, that tugs are called to assist a ship. These tough workhorses are often the heroes of the harbors, taking on massive ice breaking jobs, assisting vessels into their berths, and towing disabled ships.

Most marine construction firms on the Lakes own their own tugs and use them for moving barges and dredges within the harbors and over the lakes. One commonly found tug on construction jobs is the "towboat." Most are small, less than 40 feet long with removable deckhouses, and are easily transported by trucks. These shallow-draft, twin-screw push boats are perfect for handling small barges in tight quarters such as marinas, and to accommodate dock repairs.

In the past ten years, an increasing number of "Gulf-style" twin-screw tugs have found their way into the Lakes. Most are less than 70 feet long. These model bow twin-screw tugs have sufficient power to handle heavily loaded scows and crane rigs. They also have room for crew quarters and galleys, which come in handy on out of town jobs.

More traditionally, the contractors have typical Great Lakes style model bow single-screw diesel tugs, built between the 1930s and 1950s. The smaller 45-foot tugs are, normally, of the government Design 320 style, developed for the U.S. Army. Hundreds of these tugs were constructed, many at shipyards on the Great Lakes such as Roamer Boat Works, Sturgeon Bay Shipbuilding, and the Burger Boat Company. Construction of this incredibly successful style continued after WWII until the late 1950s. Many were built for civilian use and others were sold as surplus from either the Army or the Army Corps of Engineers. Contractors tend to like these tugs because of their power, shallow 5-foot draft, and rugged design, which make them perfect for the dredging and construction trade. They are usually found on harbor projects, tending dredges, and moving scows.

Lake towing tugs are usually at least 1,800 HP and 100 feet long. Built with deep draft and a large fuel capacity, these heavy tugs are capable of handling

Great Lakes Towing's City-Class tugs are scarce today. The *Gary* survives on the Erie Canal, owned by Spring Lake Excavating. Pictured in August 2000, still sporting her Towing Company colors but with a different stack marking, the tug is moored at the state dry dock in Lyons, New York. In 1934, While she was still a steamer, the Towing Company sold her to the Reiss Steamship Company which had purchased their larger Type 2 tug *Q. A. Gillmore* two years earlier. The *Gary* was renamed *Green Bay* under Reiss ownership and worked docking ships in Green Bay until 1981 when it was sold to Seaway Towing. Renamed *Oneida*, she was famous for leaving a trail of thick black smoke from her rare Kahlenberg diesel. Wellington Towing of Sault Ste. Marie bought her in 1987, renamed her *Iroquois,* and ran her until 1990. At that time, Great Lakes Towing bought out the Wellington operation, acquiring the tug back and giving it the state name *Alaska*. After a few years at the Soo, she was brought to Cleveland for storage. Three G-tugs were sold for off-Lakes use in the summer of 1999, the *Alaska* being one of them. On their way though the Erie Canal, the *Alaska*, which had just been renamed *Grouper*, was deemed inadequate, with her dinosaur of an engine, and was left behind. She remains in nice solid condition and carries no visible name, but on paper, she is still the *Grouper. Jason LaDue Photo*

rough seas. They also provide comfort for the crew with ample quarters, galley, and a large wheelhouse.

Another tug found in the harbor trade is the "canaller." This design originated in New York, where model bow tugs with fixed low, or retractable, pilothouses were built for special service on the Erie Canal. The Erie Canal, or New York State Barge Canal, is a manmade waterway that cuts east-west through the middle of New York, from Tonawanda to Waterford, including a leg from Three Rivers north to Oswego on Lake Ontario. At one time, heavy barge movements made this waterway a hot spot for commercial traffic. Today, the canal tugs are nearing extinction but pleasure boats frequently travel this beautiful route.

The canaller design is especially popular today in Chicago because of the river system there. Built to be retractable, the entire pilothouse will raise and descend on a hydraulic or air ram. This allows the tug to duck under bridges or rise to look over barges when pushing. On the rivers, these canallers are commonly used as push boats.

Found in nearly every port around the Great Lakes, the tugboat fleets carry impressive history. The next time you see one out working take a look. They are worth an in-depth examination.

The unmistakable bow of a G-tug. In Toledo, the *Montana* (1929), *Louisiana* (1917), and *Florida* (1926) rest for winter at their home dock on January 27, 1998. Heavy mat fendering is in place on the bows for pushing against ship hulls. The famous green hulls and red cabins with white and black trim have been the colors of the tugs since the company was founded in 1899.

The 1927-built *Kansas* gently pulls the steamer *John Sherwin* into its berth at the Superior Municipal dock. With her nose against the wall, and the bow tug holding the ship steady, the *Kansas* inches along, clearing the ice out of their path so the 806-foot ship can have a mooring tight against the dock. Built as a standard Type 2 steel G-tug, *Kansas* was Hull No. 57 of the Great Lakes Towing Company's own construction. Initially equipped with the standard 26 x 28-inch bore and stroke steam engine, the tug was repowered in 1958 with a 12-cylinder Cleveland diesel.

The Towing Company's *Superior* is a favorite among tug enthusiasts. Built as the *Richard Fitzgerald* in 1912 for the Chicago Lighterage Company, the big lake tug later worked for Kelly Island Lime, T. L. Durocher, Whitney Brothers, and Merritt Chapman & Scott before she was bought by the Towing Company in 1946. Her original means of propulsion was a massive fore and aft compound steam engine with 18- and 38-inch diameter cylinders and a 30-inch stroke. This engine was replaced in 1953 when the tug was reconstructed, giving her a "G-tug" look and an EMD 12-567A engine. Early on, the tug was adorned with a huge steam smoke stack and superstructure with a tall upper pilothouse. She was given her present name upon purchase in 1946. In 1960, the tug was repowered again, with a C-block 567, producing 1,200 HP. Manitowoc Shipbuilding built the *Superior* as Hull No. 50.

Sailing an ocean going grain ship from the Cargill B-1 Elevator in Duluth, the G-tug *Kentucky* demonstrates how its low profile design offers ease in handling while working under the giant flared bows of foreign freighters. The deckhands can be seen taking up the towline along the deck. A short bowline would have been used to steer the ship out of its berth backwards. Now that the ship is in the harbor, the tug captain slowly pushes it around, heading for the channel, while his crew puts the towing gear away, as it is lowered down from the ship. Once secured and the ship is aiming the right direction, the *Kentucky* will back off and the ship will be on its way with a belly full of grain, bound for a foreign country.

Through the years, the Towing Company has acquired several tugs that are not "true" G-tugs through buy-outs. One such boat is the *North Carolina*, built for U.S. Steel's Michigan Limestone Division. She was purchased in 1990 for ship docking and ice breaking at U.S. Steel's Rogers City terminal. By 1981, the tug had been laid up as the towage demands in the port were down. Sold to Gaelic Tug in 1983, the vessel was refit, renamed *Wicklow,* and stationed at Cleveland with the *Kinsale*. Built with a 12-cylinder 278A Cleveland, typical engine for 1950's construction, the tug has a DC electric propulsion system. Known to be good in the ice, the *North Carolina* has spent the majority of her time stationed in Duluth, typically working only during ice-breaking operations. She is pictured here assisting the steamer *John G. Munson* into its lay-up berth at Fraser Shipyards in Superior on December 31, 2000.

Another tug acquired by the Towing Company in later years is the 4,000-HP *Triton*. Built in 1941 for the U.S. Navy as the USS *Tuscarora AT-77*, the tug was later redesignated *ATA-245* in 1958. The ocean-going tug was decommissioned in 1961 and later sold for civilian service. The tug has been used on the Great Lakes to power the cement barge *St. Marys Cement*. She is pictured at Cleveland on March 17, 2000 shortly after her sale to Great Lakes Towing and still in her cement trade colors. After seeing limited service on the Lakes, the *Triton* left in September 2002 with the drill ship *Louis J. Goulet*, bound for Walker's Cay in the Bahamas. Currently the tug is in ocean service for the Puerto Rico Towing & Barge Company, a subsidiary of Great Lakes Towing.

Upon repowering from steam to diesel, the G-tug's brass vertical tube steam whistles were replaced with air horns. A set of twin Leslie Tyfon A-200 horns are a common sight on the tugs today. Developed in the 1930s for use on locomotives, the 200s were brought into marine use shortly after and became a popular horn on large tugboats and small ships. Producing a throbbing deep tone, these Tyfons are known to be some of the most powerful horns heard in the harbor. Tyfons used in the marine industry are typically solid bronze, whereas their railroad counterparts are often cast aluminum. The set pictured are on the 1911 vintage G-tug *Minnesota*, stationed at Duluth.

The popular Cleveland Diesel was made by General Motors at their Cleveland, Ohio, plant, for use in submarines. This powerful diesel engine, model 278A, is a common sight in large tugboats. Almost all G-tugs, during their repowerings from steam, received 12-cylinder 278A Clevelands. They have 100 HP per cylinder, turn relatively slowly (at about 750 RPM), and burn about 3 gallons of fuel per hour per cylinder. This particular engine, a 16-cylinder unit, is shown in the tug *Robin Lynn*. This tug, a twin to Gaelic's *Patricia Hoey, Galway Bay,* and *Carolyn Hoey*, was built at the Alexander Shipyard in New Orleans in 1952. It was originally powered by an EMD 12-567A, but was repowered in 1985 with this second-hand Cleveland.

A tugboat's worst enemy: the thruster. Pictured here is the bow thruster on Algoma Central's 730-foot bulk freighter *Algontario*. Normally well below the water's surface, the unit is visible when the ship is pumped "high and dry" for lay-up. These thrusters are propellers mounted in a through-hull tube, at the bow and/or stern, and enable the ship to maneuver sideways. The thruster units are usually powered by 400- to 800-HP diesel or electric engines and when put into use, usually eliminate the need for tugboat assistance. Even though metal grating is in place to keep debris from jamming the unit, slush ice can still be troublesome during the winter months.

Moored near the marine museum in South Haven is the small tug *Wilhelm Baum*, which was built by Speddon Shipbuilding at Baltimore, Maryland, in 1923. This 50-foot tug was purchased by Dean King of Holland in the 1960s and modified for the construction trade. Renamed *Julie Dee* in 1965, she was originally named *Captain A. Canfield* and built for the Corps of Engineers. The tug received its current name in 1974.

Purvis Marine's *Adanac* eases in to take the bowline from the ocean cargo ship *Rubin Lark* above the Soo Locks on June 22, 2003. Built in 1913, this 80-foot tug was originally powered by a steeple compound steam engine built by the Western Dry Dock Company. While owned by Consolidated Dredging, the tug became stranded off the Batchawana River on June 8, 1954. It was released 5 days later, sank off Corbeil Point, and was abandoned. Originally named *Edward C. Whalen,* she lay on the bottom of the Lake for more than three years before salvage crews finally raised her on July 5, 1957. Another nine years passed and in 1966 the tug was reconstructed, repowered to diesel, and renamed *John McLean* for her new owner, ABM Marine. She was given her present name in 1995 and is in service at Sault Ste. Marie, Ontario.

Built in Buffalo in 1901, the *Rocket* is an example of a tug that participated in the evolution of the fish tug. Built for commercial fishing service, her lifting equipment was removed in the late 1910s and the tug resumed a career in towing that has taken her through seven owners, all of which kept her original name. The tug is shown in Purvis colors at the Sault Ste. Marie, Ontario, yard. After repowering from steam, the tug ran with a C-6 Kahlenberg until 1984 when a pair of 8-71 Detroits were put in its place. Purvis Marine has owned the tug since 1969.

One of the better-known tugs on the Lakes was the *Sachem* of the Dunbar & Sullivan fleet, which sank on December 18, 1950 in Lake Erie off Dunkirk taking her 12-man crew with her. The specific cause of this mysterious sinking was never determined. Merritt Chapman & Scott raised the tug on October 22, 1951 with their derrick boat *Cherokee*. The *Sachem* was built as the steamer *John Kelderhouse* at Buffalo by the renowned tug-builder Benjamin Cowles. Her salvaged Sutton Brothers fore and aft compound steam engine, built in 1893, was taken from the tug *Sandy Hook*. This 14 and 32-inch x 22-inch bore and stroke, 300-HP engine was removed in 1950 when a 1,200-HP EMD 567 diesel was put in. This tug was sold in 1990 to Egan Marine and renamed *Derek E.* Having been laid up for several years, the tug is pictured at their shipyard facility in April 2002. It can be noted her bulwarks have been raised a couple feet on the bow and the after portion of her main deckhouse has been cut away to allow room for a towing machine.

The Sturgeon Bay Shipbuilding & Dry Dock Company built the *Owen M. Frederick* for the U.S. Army Corps of Engineers. This 65-foot tug is in service at Sault Ste. Marie and is used to move crane barges and scows involved in harbor and lock maintenance. Her 5-cylinder Kahlenberg oil engine was replaced in 1981 with a Caterpillar 3412. She is pictured downbound with the Corps crane rig *Harvey*, just above the locks, on June 18, 1997. Removal of her old style lifeboat is about the only cosmetic change this classic tug has seen since her construction in 1942.

Selvick's *Baldy B.* is pictured here assisting the steamer *Lewis G. Harriman* around the bends in the tight rivers of Milwaukee on September 6, 1993. Built as the *G. F. Becker* by the famed Toledo builder Hans Hansen in 1932, this 62-foot steel boat was originally a Detroit River mail boat, used to deliver the mail to passing steamships. It was retired in 1951 and soon after converted to a towing tug, but retained its original cabin, giving it an unusual look for a tug. Working for Frank Becker and later Gaelic Tug, the vessel remained in Detroit until 1982 when it was sold to Curly Selvick of Sturgeon Bay. Today the tug remains in service out of South Chicago, owned by John Selvick. *Jon LaFontaine photo*

Marine Tech's 1910 vintage tugboat *Callie M.* plows through the waves inside the Duluth harbor on May 8, 2002. Strong winds and heavy seas out in the Lake have made harbor conditions too rough to work. After towing her dredge into a sheltered area, the *Callie* heads home and will enjoy a day off. Built as a fish tug by the American Shipbuilding Company at Lorain, the vessel was converted to a towing tug after being purchased by the England Towing Company of Duluth in 1941. The tug was sold to Zenith Dredge in 1945 and carried its original name of *Chattanooga* until 1979 when it was repowered.

Callie M. has her stern pulled out of the water in order to change wheels. Her bow is ballasted down and a crane gently sets her stern down on the beach, so crews can easily access her shaft. Her original 1910 riveted steel hull has since been covered up with welded doubler plate. The *Callie* is Marine Tech's primary tug for moving scows and construction barges on western Lake Superior.

Docked in downtown Port Colborne, Ontario, in November 1999 is the tug *Colinette*, built by Russel Brothers in 1943. Originally owned by the Canadian Government, she was initially named *Ottawa*. The tug was sold to Oka Sand & Gravel in 1957 and re-named *Lac Ottawa*. She was given her present name in 1966. In 1975, a pair of Caterpillar D-353 diesels replaced her original 6-cylinder Vivian engine. In 2001, the tug was hauled out at Nadro Marine's Port Dover shipyard and reconstructed. Her entire superstructure was removed and a new one was constructed, which included an upper level wheelhouse. *Jason LaDue photo*

One of the larger Alligator Tugs is the *Onaman*, built in 1938 at Owen Sound by Russel Brothers. She is pictured here at Thunder Bay. The Gators were built to fulfill a need for a powerful truckable tug to be used on the inland lakes of Canada, in the logging trade. These small but stout tugs were capable of winching themselves over land and ice and served mainly in moving pulp wood on the inland waters. The unique bow of an Alligator was designed to lead wires from the tug's winch out to the log rafts. A large winch would be found ahead of the engine, below the pilothouse.

A class of Large Tugs (LT) was built for the U.S. Army in the 1940s for unlimited ocean service. LT-821 was built at Point Pleasant, West Virginia, by Marietta Manufacturing and launched in 1945. Powered by a Skinner Uniflow 3-cylinder steam engine, this giant tug was sold into civilian service after only one year in operation for the U.S. Army Quartermaster Corps. Renamed *Brooklyn* and later *Lee Reuben,* the tug saw several owners before being purchased by Escanaba Towing in 1970 and bought into the Lakes, still powered by her 24–1/2 x 24-inch bore and stroke steam plant. It was sold in 1973 to Hannah Marine Corporation to move oil barges on the Lakes and finally repowered in 1977 with a pair of EMD 16-567c diesels (3,200-HP). Renamed *Mary E. Hannah* in 1975, the tug is still in service, along with her LT fleetmates *James A. Hannah* and the now-retired *Kristen Lee Hannah*. *Photo courtesy of the Northeastern Maritime Historical Foundation*

An exciting moment at the finish line of the 2003 Detroit River Tugboat Race! Gaelic's 110-foot icebreaking tug *Roger Stahl* creeps past McDonald Marine's vintage *Dover* and another Gaelic tug, the *Shannon*. A crewmember of the *Dover* can be seen extending a pole out from the bow, in an attempt to increase the length of his tug at the finish line. Gaelic's big twin screw *Stahl* made a surprising win against the *Shannon*, which is known to be one of the fastest tugs on the Great Lakes. Roger Stahl himself, the vessel's namesake, is onboard as Chief Engineer and at the time of this photo, was in the engine room working the governors to get every last RPM out of her two EMD main engines. One of the closest races in a long time, the 2003 race was the 27th annual event, which takes place every year near Windsor near the end of June. The *Roger Stahl* was built in 1944 as the U.S. Coast Guard's *WYTM-61 Kaw*. Constructed with cut-away bows, an electric propulsion unit, and twin main engine generators, these WYTM-class tugs were built to assist vessels during heavy ice conditions in the Great Lakes and Northeast regions.

The 1939 Gulfport tug *Seneca* stands by at the steamer *J. B. Ford's* bow in 2001 at Superior. Built as the *General* but renamed *Raymond Card* the same year, the tug was requisitioned in September 1940 by the U.S. Navy and assigned to submarine net tending duties in Guantanamo Bay, Cuba for the duration of the war. She served as the USS *Keshena* YTM-731. Decommissioned and transferred to the Maritime Commission in 1946, the tug was resold to the Card Towing Company the following year and chartered to McAllister. She was given the name *Mary L. McAllister*, which she carried until her sale to the Lakes. McAllister purchased the tug in February 1950 and ran her out of Norfolk most of its life. In 1981 Chicago's North American Towing Company (NATCO) bought the tug along with another Independent tug from Philly and ran them both to the Lakes. She worked sparingly and when NATCO closed its operations in 1991, the tug was sold to Billington Contracting in Duluth.

Seneca is shown here assisting the tug *W. N. Twolan* and its tow of three empty lumber barges out of their slip, stern first, in Superior. The tug's deckhand stands around the corner of the lower cabin, clear of the towline, which would be a deadly weapon if it snapped. Wooden nameboards, a tall smoke stack, and a large bell are standard on most classic tugboats. In recent years, the *Seneca* has worked for Zenith Tug of Duluth, performing ice breaking and general towing. She is powered by her original 12-567A EMD engine, which was rebuilt in the 1980s and converted to a C-block. The tug retains its original DC electric propulsion system and tongue and groove woodwork throughout her cabins.

During WWII, a modern harbor tug was designed to replace aging steel and wood tugs requisitioned at the start of the war. They were beautiful 101-foot model bow tugs originally designated "YTB" for "Yard Tug–Big." They were all later redesignated "YTM" as in "Yard Tug–Medium." Hundreds of these tugs were immediately constructed, the majority of them completed in 1944. Many had short-lived careers with the military and were auctioned off into civilian service. Others were placed into reserve fleets for potential future use. Some were left overseas after wartime operations. Others remained in service until the 1970s when a newer class of YTBs was built. One of the WWII YTBs to escape in her original state was the USS *Connewango* YTB-388, built by Consolidated Shipbuilding at Heights, New Jersey. Purchased by the Gaelic Tugboat Company in 1977, the tug was brought into the Lakes via the Erie Canal for service at Detroit as the *Shannon*. Her original pair of 6-cylinder Cleveland diesel generators were replaced in 1980 by a pair of Cat D-398s, operated through the original Farrel-Birmingham double reduction gear. Often considered one of the prettiest tug designs of the diesel era, these YTBs swing a 114-inch wheel and are known to be quite fast.

A predecessor to the Army's 45-foot Small Tug (ST), the *Oatka* is typical of the pre-war dredge tenders built in Duluth for the Corps of Engineers. These simple, steel 40 x 10 x 4 tugs are easy on the eyes, with their riveted cabin and hull, sleek lines, classic round stack, and wood frame windows. Several were built and nearly all still exist. Marine Iron & Ship Building constructed these tugs from a design that was produced in the late 1920s, for a grocery launch hull that was about 4 feet shorter. Originally, the tugs had 2-cylinder Fairbanks-Morse oil engines but most were later repowered with 6-71 Detroit diesels. The *Oatka* was no exception and received her Gray Marine 6-71 in the early 1950s. The *Oatka* was renamed *Gull* in the late 1970s after being decommissioned from the Corps. Renamed again in 1990, she was known as the *Miss Midway* until the original name was restored in 1995. Her current owner, Acme Marine Services, purchased the vessel from Midway Oil in 1993. Today, she is powered by a turbocharged Perkins diesel. Pictured here in July 1999, the tug sits idling, tied alongside her fleetmates, the Duluth bumboats *Marine Supplier* and *Marine Trader*.

A standard U.S. Army ST, the *Houghton,* was built by Port Houston Iron Works in 1944. Launched as *ST-573*, the tug saw virtually no service with the Army and was transferred shortly after delivery to the Corps of Engineers. Based in Duluth, she saw a lifetime of service towing scows and tending the steamers *Coleman* and *Gaillard* on dredging and construction projects. Decommissioned in 1992, the tug was sold at auction to Billington Contracting. Powered by a Detroit 8v-71, the tug is still in service at Duluth. Shown on a cold November day in 2001, the tug has always kept its Corps livery.

Sturgeon Bay Shipbuilding & Dry Dock Company was one of many yards contracted to build Design 320 ST tugs for the U.S. Army. One such tug, the 45-foot *Sturshipco* was built in 1943, for the yard itself, as a tender. Renamed *Bayship* in 1968, the tug continues to provide assistance around the Bay Shipbuilding yard in Sturgeon Bay. Often, the larger tugs are just too big to work in tight quarters and that's when the *Bayship* comes in handy. The tug's light draft enables her to tow large freighters into the dry docks without disturbing the blocking set in place at the dock's bottom. The tug is also able to fit between the ship and the dock facing, inside the dry dock, to flush out ice during the winter months before the gate is closed. The tug is pictured here on March 21, 1997, breaking ice outside the shipyard's graving dock in preparation for spring fit-out.

The *Empire State* was built from the Equitable Equipment Company's ST plans at their Madisonville, Louisiana, yard in 1951. Many of these handy little tugs were built for the Great Lakes Dredge & Dock Company, which assigned them all state nicknames. Sold to Lake Michigan Contractors in the mid-1990s, the *Empire* is shown here at the Holland yard with fleetmates *Capt. Barnaby* and *Captain Roy* on April 13, 2002. Showing the wear and tear of her trade, with a dented cabin and beat-up visor, the *Empire* has lived a lifetime shifting dredges and towing mud scows on the Great Lakes. Similar in design, the *Captain Roy* was constructed at Sturgeon Bay Shipbuilding. She was built for the Corps of Engineers in 1940 and originally named *Holland*.

The Corps of Engineers *Duluth* is photographed at her homeport of Kewaunee on September 17, 1997. *Duluth* is an example of the 70-foot class of U.S. Army ST tugs. Built in 1954 by Missouri Valley Bridge & Iron Works at Leavenworth, she was originally named *ST-2015*. Transferred to the Corps in 1962, the tug worked in the Corps fleet at Duluth and later Kewaunee until being retired in 1999. The tug was transferred to the Barrien County Sheriff to be used as a dive boat. Plans did not materialize and the vessel was sold at auction in 2000. Great Lakes Dock & Material of Muskegon repowered the tug with a KT-38 Cummins and has placed the vessel back in service, keeping her Corps name, *Duluth*.

Luedtke Marine Contracting purchased the tug *Two Rivers* in 1989. Today, she is one of only two Design 327 ST tugs on the Great Lakes in their original configuration. Built in 1943 for the U.S. Army, the tug was completed at a cost of $256,000. Simply named *ST-527*, she was launched at Harvey, Louisiana, by the Allen Boat Company, one of dozens of 86-foot ST type boats built for the war effort. In 1955, she was transferred to the Corps of Engineers and put into service, working out of Kewaunee. The tug was retired in 1982, still equipped with her original 800-HP Enterprise direct reversing engine. She is pictured in March 1999, moored alongside the sunken hull of the Laker *Tampico* at Luedtke's home dock in Frankfort.

In 1995, the Duluth-based Corps of Engineers fleet received the USS *Natchitoches* YTB-799 from the U.S. Navy. Southern Shipbuilding had built her in 1968 at Slidell, Louisiana. Rechristened *D. L. Billmaier*, the tug replaced the aging *Lake Superior*, which was built as an Army LT (Large Tug) in 1943. The Corps *Billmaier* is an example of the 1960s replacement to the WWII-style YTB. More than 100 of these tugs have been constructed for the U.S. Navy at various shipyards around the country, including the Christy Corporation and Marinette Marine on the Great Lakes. They were used for general towing and ship docking at all the U.S. Naval bases. In the early 1990s, the Navy began to outsource its towing and these tugs were declared surplus. Presently, very few remain active with the Navy. Most of these YTBs were powered with opposed-piston Fairbanks Morse diesels. The *Billmaier* is one of a handful powered by 12-cylinder 645 EMDs.

Spending the last 60 years as a crane barge, the tugboat *Menasha* began life in 1926 at the yards of the Marine Iron & Shipbuilding Company in Duluth. Constructed for the U.S. Army Corps of Engineers for service on the Fox River, the 100-foot steam-powered river tug was retired after a short career, sold surplus and reduced to a barge. Pushing her in this May 2003 view is the small tug *Bee Jay*. It is rumored that this tug was constructed at the same time the *Menasha* was converted, using materials from *Menasha's* tugboat superstructure. Gallagher Marine Construction out of Escanaba owns the pair.

Buffalo's legendary fire tug *Edward M. Cotter* shows off her nice lines, fresh paint, and spotless decks on March 18, 2003. The tug gained status as a National Historic Landmark on July 4, 1996 and is still in service as an icebreaker for the City of Buffalo. The *Cotter* was constructed in 1900 by Nixon & Lewis at Elizabeth, NJ for the Buffalo Fire Department. The tug was decommissioned as a fire tug in 1992 and transferred to the Department of Public Works. Launched as the *W. S. Grattan*, she was briefly renamed *Firefighter* in 1953 before her present name was designated the same year.

The former Chicago fire tug *Joseph Medill* awaits her fate in the quaint commercial fishing port of Algoma in August 2003. Having served proudly for 40-plus years for the Chicago Fire Department, the vessel was sold for scrap in 1999. In January of that year, the vessel arrived in mint condition at 104th Street in South Chicago, where she was stripped of her machinery; six months later, she was a gutted mess. Sold to John Selvick in November 1999, the tug was towed to Sturgeon Bay for conversion to an excursion boat. Another former Chicago fire tug, the *Fred Busse,* which had already been converted, was purchased instead and the *Medill* was towed back to South Chicago in 2000. In the fall of 2002, she was towed back to Sturgeon Bay, the town she was built in by the Christy Corporation in 1949. Donated by Capt. Selvick to a dive club that year, it was cleaned for sinking and towed by a fish tug to Algoma, where it sat until 2004. Permits were denied and the vessel was sold to Basic Marine, and towed to Escanaba, likely for scrap. An exciting career as a Chicago fire tug came to an abrupt end when the *Medill* found herself being towed here and there, unwanted in every port where she arrived.

Chicago's Holly Marine Towing has a versatile fleet of modernized tugs equipped to handle river, harbor, or cross-lake work. The *Margaret Ann* is shown here at their 104th Street yard on the Calumet River on April 8, 1996. The tug began life in 1954 as Great Lakes Dredge & Dock Company's *John A. McGuire*. Sold to Gaelic Tugboat in 1987, it was renamed *William Hoey* and performed ship-docking duties in Detroit. Originally powered by a Cleveland diesel, this tug was reconstructed by Holly Marine in 1999, with the addition of a raised pilothouse and a 12-cylinder EMD.

Built for the U.S. Coast Guard as ice-breaking tugs, these WYTM-class steel tugs were constructed with cut-away bows specially designed for ice breaking and have 3/4-inch hull plate. Gulfport Boiler & Welding Works built the *WYTM-90 Arundel* at Port Arthur, Texas, in 1938. Although they are not of the same class, the *Arundel* was Gulfport Hull No. 129 and the *Seneca*, featured earlier in this book, was Gulfport Hull No. 131. After being decommissioned, the *Arundel* was sold to Canonie and renamed *Karen Andrie*. Basic Marine bought the tug in 1990 and she is pictured at their Escanaba headquarters in March 1997. Many of these tugs remain in civilian service on the Lakes. Sister ships include the *Apalachee* (Rochester), *Manitou* (Port Huron), *Roger Stahl* (Detroit), and *Jimmy L.* (Sturgeon Bay). Basic Marine also owns the *Danicia*, which began life as the *WYTM-96 Chinook*.

Thunder Bay Tug Service's *Point Valour* is a beautiful 100-foot tug used in the ship docking trade at the Canadian Lakehead. Powered by an 8-cylinder opposed-piston Fairbanks Morse, this 1,400-HP tug is in immaculate condition inside and out. She was constructed in 1958 at the Davie Shipyards in Lauzon, Quebec. Originally built for Foundation Maritime, a well-known towing and salvage firm, this tug was named *Foundation Valour* until given her present name in 1983. Docked at the company's home pier in Thunder Bay on August 11, 2002, the tug rests with fleetmate *Glenada*, moored just astern of her.

Anchored in the bay at Penetanguishene, Ontario, is the old *Georgian Storm*, a tug that began life in Sorel, Quebec, in 1931 for Marine Industries, Ltd. Built as the *Capitaine Simard* with a fore and aft compound steam engine, the tug was rebuilt in the 1950s, repowered with two Detroit 12v-71 diesels and renamed *Rene Simard*. In 1986, the tug was sold to a private party and towed by the fish tug *W. A. Spears* to Penetanguishene, where it has been inactive for many years.

John Selvick's *John A. Perry* is moored at Calumet River Fleeting's home dock in South Chicago in this April 2001 photo. Liberty Dry Dock built the 70-foot tug in Brooklyn in 1954 for the City of New York's Department of Sanitation. Originally named the *Sanita*, the tug was brought to the Lakes in 1981 and renamed *Susan M. Selvick* at Sturgeon Bay. She has been stationed in Chicago since 1992 and was given her present name in 1998. The small pilothouse in this photo had replaced a more traditional, taller one in 2000. A "step" in her stern cabin is visible, where a portion of the aft cabin was removed during a repowering. Her original tall smoke stack was also removed at that time.

Built by Fred Socie of Toledo, the *Bessie B*'s futuristic design, rounded cabins, and sloping lines make her one of the more unique looking boats on the Lakes. This 52-foot tug has worked around the Toledo area most of its life. Built in 1947, the tug was supposedly lengthened by 10 feet during a reconstruction in 1952.

One of the nicest canallers around, the *Buckley* spins around in the Calumet River, preparing to shuffle some rafted barges along the riverbank. Built as the *Linda Brooks* in 1958 by Parker Brothers at Houston, the tug was purchased by Barnaby in 1967 and renamed *Eddie B*. The twin-screw tug originally had a pair of Cat 398 diesels, which were replaced in 1984 with two Cat 3512's. In this January 2002 view, her pilothouse can be seen in the fully raised position. The deckhand is standing by the housing into which the pilothouse rests when lowered. Her twin smoke stacks are the sign of two main engines and under silver tarps on her bow, two winches are mounted for the facing wires, which are hung over the bow. These wires are placed on the corner bitts of a barge after the tug has faced up to it. The wires are tightened with the winches, making a secure connection for pushing. Her stern is sitting very deep in the water, leaving minimal freeboard. This is usually the mark of ballast in the stern tank. The deeper a tug's wheel is in the water, the less cavitation the vessel will experience, thereby increasing the torque on the wheel and creating better steerage. Tugs' hatches and doors are sealed up tight. Having their decks awash in the seas is common and typically harmless.

A canaller in action; Empire Harbor's *Cheyenne* has her bow against a ship putting a line on, in preparation to sail her from her berth on the Hudson River. *Cheyenne's* pilothouse is in the raised position, extended up high above her smoke stack and fittings for maximum visibility. A beautiful boat all around, the *Cheyenne* was built by Ira Bushey in 1965. This Brooklyn tug builder was considered one of the best. Originally named *Glenwood* for the Red Star line, the tug has spent her life moving oil barges on the East Coast and New York State Barge Canal. A strong 10-cylinder Fairbanks Morse opposed-piston diesel engine powers the *Cheyenne*.

The few canallers that remain are maintained with pride and the *Sharon Elizabeth* is no exception. The 1,200-HP *Sharon* is pictured on February 25, 2003 at Georgetown with her paint and decks in immaculate condition and tires neatly hung. In this image, her telescoping pilothouse can be seen in a partially raised position. In its extreme low position, the pilothouse windows would be completely buried in the housing and the captain would look through the portholes in the cabin to navigate. As with all canallers, her masts and smoke stack are built no taller than the pilothouse in its lowered position. Built for Moran as the *Thomas E. Moran*, the tug was requisitioned for the war and served with the U.S. Navy as the USS *Namontack* YTB-738 until returned to Moran in 1947. The tug is now part of the McAllister Towing fleet in South Carolina. DeFoe Boat & Motor Works built *Sharon* at Bay City in 1938. She measures 90 x 25 feet with a 10-foot draft and is powered by a 12-278A Cleveland with a DC electric propulsion unit.

General Marine's *Hannah D. Hannah* is busy spotting coke barges in this November 2002 scene at Gary. A twin-screw canaller, she has been outfitted with a tow-knee on her bow and electric deck winches for facing wires when pushing barges. The captain controls the winches by simply pushing a button to tighten the cables once the crew has placed the eyes of the cables over the barge's bitts. Her hailer speaker, air horn, and spot lights can all be seen mounted below the pilothouse roofline, to further reduce the tug's height, or "air draft," after the pilothouse has been lowered. The radar unit is also mounted on a fold-down stand, so it too can be dropped out of the way of low bridges. The *Hannah D.* was built in Sturgeon Bay in 1956 and has spent her life working out of South Chicago, under various names including *Harbor Ace, Gopher State,* and later, *Betty Gale.*

"Towboats" or "pushboats" are commonly found on the inland rivers. These tugs are usually built on a flat, barge-like hull with a square bow and tall pushing knees in place. They are most always found pushing their tow, faced up to a barge (or barges), and connected to them with facing wires. This tug, the *J. H. Tanner*, is typical of those found on the Great Lakes. Ports such as Chicago are fed by major river systems and receive thousands of barges each year, which need to be moved to their appropriate loading and unloading destinations. Tugs like the *Tanner*, built like canallers with retractable pilothouses, are useful for breaking up the big river tows upon arrival and bringing the barges down to the Calumet River where fleeting companies take over.

Calumet River Fleeting's *Des Plaines* is a 100-foot canal style towboat used in South Chicago. The tug was retired in recent years, but is pictured here in June of 1996 at Chicago's 104th Street slip, moving coal barges. She is powered by two rare Baldwin-Lima-Hamilton diesels. Built in 1956 by St. Louis Shipbuilding & Steel Company, she is one of the last first-generation diesel towboats on the Lakes.

The stout 32-foot-wide *Steve A. McKinney* is a modern, tough towboat powered by a pair of V16-149 Detroit diesels. This 1,800-HP, 85-foot long canaller has a retractable pilothouse that will go up "to the moon," according to her former captain. It is pictured here in the lowered position in Chicago Harbor's North Slip, which is used for fleeting barges. Fleeting is a term applied to mooring and sorting barges while they are in port. The *McKinney* has come in behind a Hannah tug to pull out a couple of barges that were waiting their turn for loading.

Another type of canaller, unique to the New York State Barge Canal system, is the state owned *Syracuse*. Built in Syracuse in 1934, this 75-foot tug has spent her career under the employ of the New York State Department of Transportation. These tugs are specially designed to have sufficient power for towing heavy barges and dredges and still have light draft and low air draft, in order to fit under the 15-foot bridges along the Erie Canal from Syracuse to Buffalo. Powered by a Cat diesel, the *Syracuse* is typical of the state tugs; she is well kept and reflects the pride of her crew throughout. The tug is built with virtually no sheer, a flat barge-like deck, model bow, rounded stern, and the standard capstan, quarter, and H-bitts. She is pictured between jobs at Mud Lock, on the Cayuga-Seneca Canal on June 20, 2002.

Kadinger Marine's *David J. Kadinger* heads outbound the Calumet River in South Chicago. Her old name, *N. F. Candies*, can still be seen welded on the bow. Built in 1969 at Lockport, Louisiana, by Bollinger Marine, the 65-foot twin-screw 1,000-HP tug spent her early years working in the Gulf before being brought into the Lakes in 1989.

Built in Bourg, Louisiana, in 1978, the *Douglas B. Mackie* came to work on the Lakes for Great Lakes Dredge & Dock in 1990. Powered by twin Detroit 16v-149 diesels, the design of this 2,200-HP twin-screw general towing tug has become an industry standard in the construction trade. The versatility of these high-horsepower twin-screw vessels allow them to handle heavy crane barges and loaded mud scows with ease in tight quarters and unfavorable weather conditions. The *Mackie* is pictured here at GLD&D's South Chicago yard in 1995.

J. J. Camalick & Sons built the Eleanor M. in Chicago in 1992 for use as a tender (small tug used for a general workboat). She has a fish tug style hull that measures 35 x 10 feet. Powered by a Detroit 6-71, this single screw workboat was sold in 1999 to Buffalo Industrial Diving and renamed *Deep See*. It is in service at Buffalo as a workboat in the commercial diving business. On January 1, 2002, a heavy snowfall piled so much snow on the deck of this small tug moored in the Buffalo River that it sank at the dock. The tug was raised the following week and repaired.

Roen Salvage is a construction firm based in Sturgeon Bay that has become well known throughout the years for their completion of difficult salvage tasks around the Lakes. One of their tugs, the *Stephan M. Asher*, is moored in Racine in this September 2002 photo. Used truck tires line the hull, making adequate fendering to protect itself from friction between docks or barges they are towing. Burton Construction built the *Stephan* at Port Arthur, Texas, for Texaco Oil in 1954. Beautiful wood frame windows and the wooden nameboard below are a rare sight on tugs these days. Floodlights are visible on the main deckhouse to light up the working area on the bow. Against her cabin are four fuel tank vent pipes. Tugboat fuel tanks are usually located in the hull, below the pilothouse.

In September 2000, an unusual tug arrived on the Lakes from the Arctic. The *Radium Yellowknife,* along with her nine *Radium*-series barges, was employed on the McKenzie River until Buchanan Forest Products purchased them for use on Lake Superior. The nine barges were brought in, stacked on top of each other, in sets of threes. Used for hauling lumber from Thunder Bay to Superior, the entire fleet went into lay-up after running two years. She is pictured here inbound the Superior harbor entrance on June 19, 2001, still in her former owner's colors. The *Yellowknife* was built by Yarrow's Limited in 1948 at Vancouver. She measures 120 feet long and is powered by two Cat D-398 diesels.

The East Coast harbor tug *Brian A. McAllister* was chartered in 1963 by Wilson Marine Transit to power the barge *Horace S. Wilkinson,* which was a converted Laker. Returning to the coast after only one season, the 1961-built *Brian A.* remains a useful harbor tug, based at Staten Island. She is pictured on March 8, 2002, preparing to sail the container ship *Atlantic Conveyor* from its berth in the Port of Newark. The "doghouse" atop her pilothouse allows the captain better visibility when pushing barges with high freeboard or tall loads. While on charter to Wilson, a large upper pilothouse was added, raising the line of sight about 16 feet. That structure was later removed and then in the late 1990s this smaller setup was added.

The *Jane Ann IV* has backed out of her notch in the barge *Sarah Spencer* and is tied along the Cargill grain elevator in Duluth. The *Spencer* was the former steamship *Adam E. Cornelius*, and is now converted to a self-unloading barge, with her stern notched, for a tug to push. Mitsui Engineering built *Jane Ann IV* as the *Ouro Find* in Fujinagata, Japan, in 1978. The 140-foot twin-screw tug was outfitted with large hydraulic "pins" to lock her into the barge. These can be seen, just below her name, on the bow.

The tug *Presque Isle* was constructed for the single purpose of pushing its barge, also named *Presque Isle*. Together, with the tug in the notch, as shown in this photograph, the pair make up a 1,000-foot long self unloading freighter used in the iron ore trade on the Great Lakes. Halter Marine Services built the tug in 1973 at New Orleans. That same year, her barge was constructed on the Lakes at two different shipyards, and then joined together. The 15,000-HP tug *Presque Isle* is owned by Great Lakes Fleet, the operators of the former U.S. Steel steamship fleet.

A gigantic section of hull is slowly moved from the Bay Shipbuilding fabrication shop on March 21, 1997. This stern section is seeing daylight for the first time, resting on a platform moved by tracks, much like how the Space Shuttle is transported to its launch pad. The hull section was later overturned and placed into the graving dock by giant cranes where it was fitted with the bow section, which had been set into place first. The boat, named only *Hull 742* at this point, would, in less than a year's time, become Van Enkevort's 10,000-HP articulated tug *Joyce L. Van Enkevort*. Initially mated with Interlake's barge *Pathfinder* in 1998, the tug later went on to power the barge *Great Lakes Trader*, built in 1998.

Chapter 3: BARGES

The most common commercial vessel found on the Great Lakes and inland river system is the barge. Ranging in size from 20-foot work flats to 1,000-foot cargo ships, "barge" is a term that can be applied to just about any non-powered craft used in a commercial application.

Much of the bulk cargos moved on the Lakes today are being handled by barge thanks to fewer crew required on tugboats than on a steam or motor cargo ships. Several old Lakeboats have been converted into barges by notching their sterns so tugs can push the unit. Some tugs are loosely connected and once out of the tight quarters in rivers or harbors, they will cut loose and tow the barge, rather than push it. Others are locked tightly to the barge by using hydraulic rams, or pins, that lock into their notches, so they push the barges regardless of the conditions. To the operators, a positive element for these barge conversions, in addition to crewing requirements, is the ability to quickly separate the propulsion unit from the ship. In case of a breakdown, another tug could quickly be called to replace the one in need of repair. The tug can be separated from its cargo barge in a matter of minutes. These tug/barge units range in size from small 300-foot conversions to large 1,000-foot custom-built combinations.

Pictured in this chapter are several examples of ship-sized barges that are either converted steamboats or newly constructed specialty barges for Great Lakes

service. All are pushed by large, powerful tugs, of at least 5,000 HP.

Many other barges used in over-lakes transportation can be found in service today. Medium size tank barges are a common sight on the Lakes, loaded with cargos such as fuel oil or calcium chloride. Today, most tank barges are of double hull construction. In most areas, single-hull tank barges are now illegal in the oil trade because of the great number of accidents and spills in recent years.

Other barges have flat decks and are used to haul cargo or to use as work platforms in the construction business. Cargo barges tend to have raised bin walls to keep their cargo or machinery from sliding off in heavy seas.

Barges used in the construction trade are often equipped with "spuds." Spuds are tall legs that extend through pockets or "spud wells," built into the hull of the barge; they can be raised or lowered, either by crane or winch. The spuds drop down and pierce the lakebed below, holding the barge in place. Contractors can have a tug position the barge exactly where it is needed and then an operator will drop the spuds, anchoring the barge in place. Spud barges are often found with a crane secured on deck used for dredging or pile driving.

When dredging, for example, a large crane or long-reach excavator will be set on deck of a spud barge. Timber mats are anchored in place for the steel-

The *Joseph H. Thompson* was purchased from the Maritime Commission and placed into service on the Lakes following a conversion from a C-4 cargo ship to a laker after WWII. In 1985, the vessel began another extensive conversion that took more than six years to complete. In 1992, the vessel re-entered service as a self-unloading barge pushed by a diesel-electric tug powered by three General Electric diesels. The vessel is wearing Hanna colors in this photo, crossing Lake Superior, heavily loaded with ore from the Allouez docks. A small U.S. Steel steamer can be seen following. *Author's collection*

tracked excavator to sit on. The operator will spud down in the first area to be dredged (known as a "cut") and start digging. The dredged material will be put into a scow, which is usually tied alongside the Spud barge. When the operator is ready to move ahead or back, he can reposition himself without the need for a tug, by lifting one spud at a time and using the excavator's bucket to "paddle" through the water and "walk" the spud barge by swinging on the spuds.

Spud barges are used to build marinas, repair commercial dock facings, transfer cargo from disabled ships, and engage in dockside structural repair, construction, or dismantling. Some spud barges have a small structure on one end, which houses an engine room for the spud engines, a ship's generator for power, and a workshop. Some will also have a small galley or even crew quarters. This structure is referred to as a "hooch," "barn," or "house."

Other crane barges, with or without spuds, are the "derrick boats." Most derricks are flat-deck barges with large, powerful, built-in A-frames, booms, and winches for performing the same duties as Spud barges. Primarily steam powered, derricks became obsolete when the economical, diesel-powered cranes appeared. It was much easier and cheaper to rig up spud barges to take on the same duties.

In a similar story, mechanical dredges have also become a thing of the past. The mighty "dipper dredge" was once a common sight on the Lakes and was an amazing piece of equipment. Downright scary, these massive steam dinosaurs were truly a living, breathing, floating steam shovel. With creaks, moans, and the smell of oil and steam, these steel beasts would tear into the harbor or river's bottom and excavate massive amounts of sediment to maintain the required depths for navigation. Nothing can dig like a dipper, but the cost of operating a steam-powered dredge far exceeds that of operating a modern spud barge with a diesel crane and clam bucket.

The last dipper to operate on the Great Lakes was the *Duluth* of the Zenith Dredge fleet in Duluth, Minnesota. Only one unit remains, the *DD-3*, of the Erie Canal Corporation. All her machinery is built on the "light" side and is capable of folding down to maintain a 15-foot air draft. Even though the *DD-3* is of a canal variety, she is still a steam dipper.

"Scow" is a term usually applied to barges of a lower class, but in general, is just another name for a barge. Dump scows are barges, with usually, five or six cargo holds or "pockets." Mud, or "spoils," from

dredging are dumped into these pockets and when the scow is loaded, a tug tows it out to dumping grounds designated by the U.S. Army Corps of Engineers. A diesel engine powers a gearbox that turns a shaft that controls the large double doors (usually made of timber with steel frames) at the bottom of the scow. Each pocket can be dogged separately by using a handle to activate the sprocket and chain system that will lower the doors, thereby dumping the cargo through the bottom of the barge. Although dump scows are very handy to have, actual dumping hardly ever takes place now. Almost all dredged spoils are now unloaded on shore and disposed of or screened and reused as sand in the construction trade.

Another common type of barge is the "hopper." Hopper barges are typically built with one big cargo hold. Watertight bulkheads separate tanks along the sides of the barge and at the ends or "rakes." A 200-foot-long hopper barge will typically have four side tanks on each side and two rake tanks on each end. Hoppers are generally used in the river system for hauling grain, scrap, cement, coal, and ore. After they are loaded, the barges' fiberglass or steel covers can be set into place using a shoreside crane, in order to protect the cargo from the elements.

Chicago is directly connected to the Inland Rivers and receives thousands of hopper barges each year. Cargos come from or go to South Chicago's Calumet River or Lake Michigan ports such as Indiana Harbor, Burns Harbor, Gary, Holland, or Milwaukee. Local tug companies such as Calumet River Fleeting, General Marine Towing, Holly Marine Towing, Kindra Lake Towing, or Kadinger Marine are contracted to tow these barges to their final destination.

Although most ferries on the Lakes have traditionally been powered, several were non-powered barges for railway use. Some were converted from steam-powered self-propelled ferries. These large flat-decked barges were laid out with several sets of railroad tracks on deck and were used to move train cars back and forth between Detroit and Windsor before the tunnel was built.

In just about every port you visit, a barge of some sort will be found. Anyone spending time at a marina will undoubtedly have an opportunity to watch a spud barge, small or large, making dock repairs, driving piles, or performing routine dredging. Although they are, by far, the most overlooked commercial vessel, the barges have a long and fascinating history. In some cases, much more history than imagined.

The *Joseph H. Thompson*, pushed by tug *Joseph H. Thompson, Jr.,* loads at the North side of Dock No. 1 of the DM&IR Railway in Two Harbors on June 12, 1997. The cargo is a shipment of "chips" from LTV Steel. Chips are broken taconite pellets, a product generated primarily from cleaning up the stockpile yards. It is interesting to note that the original portion of the *Thompson's* C-4 hull is welded while the newer forebody is riveted. The large tug that is used to push the vessel today was constructed using steel from the ship's stern that was cut away during its conversion to a barge.

Hull No. 424 of Wisconsin's Manitowoc Shipbuilding Company began life as the steam powered Laker *Adam E. Cornelius* in 1959. She is photographed here, working for the American Steamship Company, her original owner. *Cornelius* was the last Laker built with telescoping hatches. Laid up in the 1980s, as many old steamers were, she was one of the few that escaped the scrapper's torch and was instead, sold for conversion to a tug barge unit.

The *Cornelius* emerged in 1989 as a "new" vessel, under Canadian flag. She was rechristened *Capt. Edward V. Smith*, but would soon be renamed *Sea Barge One* under new ownership. What was once a proud U.S. steam-powered Laker is now just a barge. Seen from the bow, her appearance is virtually unchanged. She is photographed unloading her cargo into the Superior General Mills elevator in July 1995.

Sea Barge One operated for only a few years under that name and was eventually renamed *Sarah Spencer*, after the owner's daughter and son. It can be noted in this photo, taken in Huron, Ohio on March 16, 1997, that her stern has been cut off and modified: a tugboat fits into and pushes in the large notch that was created. It is also easy for the tug to "cut off" from its barge in order to go take on fuel, make repairs or to perform its own ice breaking, keeping the channel clear before departure. After leaving port, some of these tug/barge units will cut loose from their notch once in open waters and tow the barge behind them on a long hawser. Depending on the unit, this can result in better handling in heavy seas. However, when in ports and rivers, the tug is so tightly locked into its notch, that together they are truly one ship. In many cases, large tugboats in this combination have more horsepower than separate ships of equal capacity.

In this aerial photo taken in October 1997, the *Sarah Spencer* is unloading into a hopper on the Cargill B-2 grain elevator in Duluth. Her tug, *Atlantic Hickory*, can be seen in the notch at the stern. This tug was built in 1973 and has a pair of EMD 20-cylinder 645-E5 diesels that produce 7,200-HP. However, the 160-foot tug has since been replaced by the tug *Jane Ann IV*, built in Fujinagata, Japan, in 1978.

Steamer *J. L. Mauthe* is at the mercy of the tugs *Kansas* and *Vermont* on December 2, 1996. She is moving from her lay-up berth in Superior into Fraser Shipyard where the hull will be prepared for towing across Lake Superior. Her final destination is Bay Shipbuilding at Sturgeon Bay, where she will undergo a conversion to a self-unloading barge. The *Mauthe* was the last untouched version of the "AAA-Class" of 647-foot bulk carriers built in 1952/1953. Others in that class; including the *Arthur M. Anderson, Armco,* and *Philip R. Clarke*, have all been lengthened and converted to self-unloaders.

It is June 1997 and the *Mauthe's* conversion is well underway. Her cabins have been removed, her tanks cleaned, and crews are now starting to cut away portions of her stern. Her entire aft end, including steam turbines and machinery, will be removed and a large notch will be cut. This notch will be "home" to a large tug, built new to push this barge.

Formerly the *J. L. Mauthe*, the barge *Pathfinder* makes her way around the bends of Cleveland's Cuyahoga River in June 1998, only one year after the previous photo. The newly constructed 10,000-HP tug *Joyce L. Van Enkevort* is in the notch, pushing. *Al Hart photo*

Laid-up in Muskegon is the old Penn Dixie Cement barge *Sea Castle*. Launched in Great Britain as the *Kaministiquia*, the tanker was constructed in 1909 for the Western Navigation Company, out of Port Arthur. She was built by the same shipyard that constructed the famed ocean liner *Mauretania* two years earlier. *Sea Castle* was converted to a cement carrier in 1929 and finally reduced to a barge in 1968. After a long lay-up, the barge was finally sold for scrap and dismantled on site in 2004. Her original triple-expansion steam plant and engine room machinery were found to be intact, below deck where her cabins had been removed decades before.

In for hull re-plating is the cement barge *Medusa Conquest*. Workers at the Bay Shipbuilding yard have lights strung along the side of this barge in preparation for working during the night. Old damaged plates are cut away from the ship, frames are repaired, and new heavy plates are set into place. Bay Ship is one of the few yards remaining that are capable of riveting ship's hulls. Large plates of steel are set into place and then pinned together with rivets; it is the same process used when the ship was constructed in 1937. A six-man crew is busy on this ship in this March 1997 photo. Three burners are on the dock, cutting plates and rub strakes to fit carefully into the side of the ship. One man is "cooking" the red-hot rivets on the deck of the ship, which are then dropped over the side into a bucket and set into their holes. Large pneumatic guns pound the rivet into place. Built by Manitowoc Shipbuilding as the *Red Crown* for Standard Oil, the petroleum tanker was converted to a cement barge in 1987. Reconfiguring its holds and shortening the vessel by 46 feet, with the addition of a notched out stern, enabled the vessel to be powered by a large tug.

This is what could, very possibly, be the future for bulk transport on the Great Lakes. The newest tug and barge unit, the *Great Lakes Trader*, is pictured loading limestone at Stoneport on September 19, 2000. She is almost brand new in this photo. Construction began in 1999 and finished in 2000 at New Orleans. The unit was towed to the Lakes in June and entered service that summer, powered by the 10,000-HP tug *Joyce L. Van Enkevort*. The *Trader* can carry just over 39,000 tons of cargo and is built with a self-unloading system much like those on the standard Great Lakes self-propelled freighters. Although the same size as most freighters, this 740-foot barge's crew is smaller, thus making it a more efficient unit to operate in today's battle for economics in Lake transportation. *Jon LaFontaine photo*

In 1996, LaFarge Cement had a new 460-foot cement barge built by Bay Shipbuilding at Sturgeon Bay. This new unit replaced at least one older self-powered steamship previously in the cement trade for the same company. The *Integrity* is pictured at the Waukegan silos on December 6, 1999. The deckhands can be seen at the bow taking out the bow wire, as she has just docked. She is being pushed by the 7,000-HP tug *Jacklyn M.*

Built by Manitowoc Shipbuilding in 1930 as the beautiful railroad ferry *City of Flint 32*, this steamship was cut down to a car ferry barge in 1969 and renamed *Roanoke*. Locomotives pushed their freight cars onto the deck of this barge, which has several sets of tracks on deck. The cars then rode across river and were pulled off into another yard on the other side. Owned by the Norfolk & Western Railway and used in service from Windsor, Ontario, to Detroit, the service had just been discontinued when this photo was taken of the vessel in lay-up at Toledo in 1994. *Wendell Wilke photo*

Many tank barges are in use around the Lakes, operated by Andrie, Hannah, and McKeil, to name a few. Most tank barges today have double skins. In other words, they have a double bottom. If the barge should strike an obstruction and tear a hole in its hull, only one tank is flooded; the vessel is in no immediate danger and the cargo will not spill out. Many of the older, single skin barges have been forced into retirement. One such barge is the 1940 vintage *Mr. Micky*, once operated by Halco Barge Lines of Green Bay. The 195-foot barge was typically found being pushed by a tug from the Selvick fleet of Sturgeon Bay. Photographed at the Basic Marine Shipyard in February 2002, the *Micky*, although still in solid condition, was no longer allowed to haul oil and was cut up for scrap in 2004. The Dravo Corporation built the barge at Neville Island, Pennsylvania.

A typical barge used on the river systems is this 195 x 35-foot barge built for American Commercial Barge Lines in 1979 by Jeff Boat Inc. at Jeffersonville, Indiana. Jeff Boat is one of the primary builders of river barges today. *ACBL-3118* is pictured in December 2002 at the port of Indiana Harbor ready to unload her cargo of scrap. Large fiberglass covers are stacked on the barge ends, leaving her open and ready for unloading. These barges, although well constructed, are more flimsy than the pre-WWII hulls and have a typical life expectancy of only about 25 years.

Ferriss Marine's 1,200-ton capacity deck barge *47* is shown here under tow of the Gaelic tug *Patricia Hoey*, which is positing the barge downtown Detroit for a fireworks display. The date is June 23, 2001 and soon the barge will be loaded with explosives for a display on the Detroit River. Ferriss's similar 175 x 40-foot barges *47* and *48* were sold for scrap in December 2004 and towed to Canada. The *47* was built in 1933 of riveted steel construction and later had cement decking put in place.

A standard Spud barge shows her basic setup when empty of machinery. Ferriss Marine Contracting's *F-103* is a 110 x 42-foot barge with massive spuds that are mounted on one side only. Formerly the *DAL 20*, the barge is photographed in the Rouge River at Detroit on June 23, 2001. Construction crews use these barges to place equipment, such as cranes, for pile driving.

The George Gradel Company of Toledo took over the old Erie Sand property in Sandusky in 1999. Pictured at this dock on June 20, 2004 is the crane barge *Derrick Boat II*. A crane barge is typically a heavily built deck barge with at least two spuds, winches, a mat to walk a crane onto, and a small superstructure, used as a tool room and lunch area. This 70 x 30-foot barge has a raked bow and an excavator is on the stern instead of a crane. The *DRKBT II* is set up, in this photo, for performing light dredging. The excavator will reach over the end and dig, and then deposit its spoils into a scow alongside.

The Edward E. Gillen Company of Milwaukee owns the *Harbor Builder*, a well fit-out crane barge. With three large spuds, a large tool and engine room, big winches, and heavy construction, this barge has ample deck room for the large Manitowoc crane she has aboard. Manitowoc Shipbuilding constructed this 150 x 45 x 12 barge in 1930. The *Builder* is photographed on the night of January 30, 1998 at Milwaukee.

The *Spud Barge 2086* is pictured at the Duluth Corps vessel yard with its American Crane on one end, containment bin amidships, and workshop on the stern. This well-equipped 100 x 34-foot crane rig was built in 1954 for the Corps. Originally named *Huron* and still referred to as such, she was given her new "paper name" in the 1990s. The barge is equipped with a full workshop, compressor room, galley, head, and two 45-foot spuds. The barge arrived in 1996 to replace the *Markus*. Her American cable crane also came off the *Markus*. Her builder is unknown, but the barge arrived in the Detroit District of the Corps in 1976.

The former Corps crane barge *Markus* is pictured here in Manistee on an environmental dredging job in 1997. The 100-foot barge was built as the *DK-20* for the U.S. Army in 1924. At the end of her Corps career, in 1996, it was transferred to the EPA for use at Manistee. Next, it went to the Michigan DNR and, soon after, was sold to Durocher. At the Durocher auction in 2002, MCM bought the barge and has placed it into civilian service. With the Corps, the unit was involved in the "mystery barrel" search in Lake Superior with the tug *Lake Superior*, recovering barrels that were disposed of by the government during WWII containing suspected toxic materials. The barrels turned out to be nothing more than munitions and other non-hazardous materials, likely more secretive than toxic. Upon leaving the Duluth Corps yard after retirement, the *Billmaier* towed her to St. Ignace, where the *Kenosha* picked her up and towed her the rest of the way to Manistee. Today the barge is equipped with a Manitowoc crane and stationed at the Sault.

Another Corps of Engineers barge, the *FLS-35,* is shown here in January 1983 with a containment wall built for use with either dredge spoils or fresh sand fill, used in harbor maintenance projects. Built by Manitowoc Shipbuilding in 1926, the 90 x 28-foot barge has a 193-ton capacity. The barge was later renamed *35* and based in the Chicago Corps fleet.

Billington Contracting has purchased many vessels from the Corps of Engineers when their surplus equipment is put up for auction. One such vessel, the *Scow 10*, is pictured here in West Duluth at Hallett Dock 7 on August 1, 2003. It is a pipeline scow, used to hold the ends of hydraulic dredge pipe ends out of the water while they are being towed. The Corps had the barge built in 1942 by the Levingston Shipbuilding Company. Since then, the vessel has been used on various projects around the Great Lakes. For one such project, she was leased as the pipe scow for TNT's big hydraulic dredge *Louise*. In 2001, Billington Contracting pulled the small barge out at its West Duluth shipyard and replated the hull.

The Merritt-Chapman & Whitney Corporation built the *Fuel Scow No. 16* at Superior in 1931. The 100 x 30-foot oil barge was the bunker fuel tender for the steam dipper dredge *Col. D. D. Gaillard*. Both were owned by the U.S. Army Corps of Engineers and stationed at Duluth. The *No. 16* would be moored alongside the *Gaillard* and a steam line attached. Using heating coils inside the barge, her cargo of bunker oil would be heated so that the product could be easily pumped into the dredge's bunkers. Sold at auction in 1991, the barge was purchased by Billington Contracting. Sidewalls were added so that the barge could be used to haul dredge spoils. Unofficially named *330* by the dredging crews, the old *No. 16* is able to carry 330 yards of spoils material. She is pictured at the Duluth Timber slip in October 2001. Behind her is the old Zenith dipper dredge *Duluth* and lying on the pier next to the barge is the cutter head and ladder off Zenith's hydraulic dredge *Superior*.

Downtown Cleveland sees its fair share of vessel action and April 17, 2001 is no exception as Lake Michigan Contractor's (LMC) canal tug *Curly B.* shoves the big mud scow *No. 59* around the bends towards Lake Erie. The tug is on charter to MCM Marine, which bought the scow from LMC the previous year. *No. 59* is a large open hopper, used for hauling dredge spoils. She measures 223 feet long by 42 feet wide and was built in 1931 by American Shipbuilding at Lorain. A modern hull for her time, most of the scows in her class are still in regular service.

Canal Corporations' barge *101* is resting on the blocks for winter in the Lyons dry dock. This barge is a five-pocket dump scow. Spoils are dug by a dredge and placed into these pockets. Once the loaded scow is towed to a dump area, the doors are lowered using large chains and sprockets, usually powered by a diesel engine. Once the mud dumps out of the barge, the doors are hoisted back into place and the scow is towed back to the dredge site for another load. Although the pockets appear small, dredge spoils are wet and heavy. Fully loaded, a dump scow will have only inches of free board.

The old Zenith Dredge Company's scow *No. 16* is pictured "on the hip" of (tied alongside) the tug *Seneca* as they depart the Allouez ore docks loaded with spoils from a dredging job. While only half the scow is visible, this close image is an interesting view of how the old dump scows are laid out. Six pockets can be filled with mud, dug by a dredge from the bottom of the harbor. The materials are loaded into these scows, which have two huge doors at the bottom of each pocket. Once in a designated disposal area, the doors are dropped open, and the load falls out of the scow. When dredging, the water in the bucket naturally drains out of the pocket through the gaps at the bottom. While dumping scows are very rare these days, they are still used and the spoils are unloaded shoreside, usually by an excavator. This particular scow is 130 feet long and was built for Zenith in 1947 at Marine Iron & Shipbuilding in Duluth. Her doors are powered by a Detroit 3-71 diesel that is mounted in the small structure, pictured at the stern of the barge.

Another Corps of Engineers barge, the *BC-6289*, has just loaded and is waiting its turn to be towed out to the Superior breakwall where crews are setting armor stone for routine maintenance and erosion control. This 120 x 33-foot barge has a heavy steel containment wall to hold its deck load. Both bow and stern have a rake, or sloping end, that makes for easier towing. A load of stone is on her deck with various orange peel and clam bucket attachments at the stern, in place for use on a crane rig that is waiting at the job site.

The Corps of Engineers steamer *Coleman* rests at its homeport of Duluth on October 28, 1997. In this aerial view, her layout can easily be seen: engine room, quarters, and galley are aft; a large open work deck in the center and a hooch forward, which house an anchor windlass and storage for fittings. Cargo holds in her tanks, under the main deck, provide additional space for stowage. The *Coleman* was built in 1923 and was the first steel hull to be constructed at Marine Iron & Shipbuilding of Duluth. This steam Derrick boat worked steady throughout her 72-year career with the Corps.

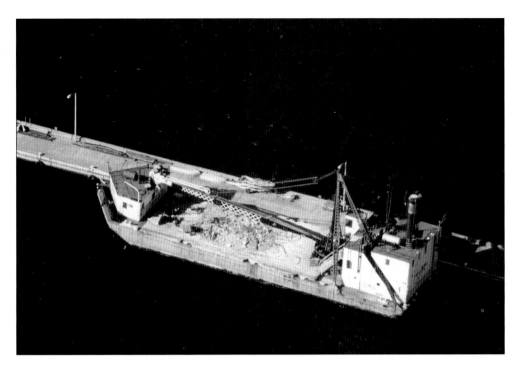

The *Coleman* was sold at auction in 1998 for scrap value. The winning bidder was Billington Contracting, which cut off the derrick and A-frame, with the idea that it would be used as a deck barge and floating workshop. In March 2000, the beautiful old derrick steamer caught fire and her entire aft superstructure was left a gutted mess. The superstructure was eventually removed, and went, with her boiler and steam engines, to the scrapyard. The *Coleman* retains her name and is in service as a dredge spoils barge with her forward structure still in place and a containment wall built around her deck.

The derrick boat *DB-2A* is moored outside the Lyons dry dock in June 2002. The Canal Corporation uses these barges for canal maintenance. The *2A* has a clam bucket attached, set up for dredging operations. Her spuds are in the lowered position, holding the vessel in place. Inside the superstructure is a galley and engine room with fuel tanks and hoists down below. Like all the other Canal dredges and derricks, the A-frame folds down to keep the vessel's height under 15 feet, in order to pass under low bridges. *Jason LaDue photo*

The Corps of Engineers barge, *Paul Bunyan,* is moored at her homeport of Sault Ste. Marie. The massive gate lifter was built in 1945 by the Wiley Equipment Company at Muskegon, which had completed a number of contracts for the government over the years at their Port Deposit, Maryland, yard. Measuring in at 150 feet long and 65 feet wide, this huge rig is used for lock maintenance at the Soo locks, but sees limited service. Built as a steam unit, the *Bunyan* originally had two 55-foot spuds and a 250-ton hoist capacity.

The Corps of Engineers crane barge, *Nicolet,* is photographed in June 2003 with the tug *Whitefish Bay* in the West Neebish Channel of the St. Mary's River. Bay Shipbuilding constructed this crane rig as Hull No. 707 in 1971. Ahead of the large Manitowoc crane is a control room. The upper level was added in the mid-1990s. Two spuds can be seen, in opposite corners of the barge. This 120 x 40 x 8-foot unit is based at Sault Ste. Marie and is used for waterway maintenance.

MCM's big Manitowoc Whirley dredge, *No. 55,* is pictured above the Soo locks on June 21, 2003, during a dredging job. The Manitowoc Shipbuilding Company built these massive Bucyrus-Erie units in 1927. She and her sister, *No. 56,* were built for Great Lakes Dredge & Dock, later sold to Lake Michigan Contractors, and then in 2001 purchased by MCM. The *56* went into lay-up, while the *55* went into immediate service. They are amazing pieces of machinery to watch when they are in action. Measuring 165 feet long by 44 feet wide, the riveted steel hull and part-wood superstructure make this dredge one of the more classic vessels in action on the Lakes. Alongside in this photo are the dredge-tending tug, *Peach State,* and spoils scow *No. 60.*

Gulfport Boiler & Welding Works built the old *ST-12*, a one-time Johnson Brothers spud barge, in 1942 at Port Arthur. The 210-foot barge has two 60-foot spuds powered by twin 6-cylinder Chrysler Commando gas engines. Later renamed *Panama*, the barge was purposely flipped over at the dock and the entire bottom was replated. Doing this made her American Bureau of Shipping (ABS) certificate unrenewable, because hulls cannot be doubled and meet the ABS standards. In this photo, she is shown in action in July 2000 for Billington Contracting on a Duluth harbor dredging project. Sidewalls have been built to hold spoils and a work pad was added for a large Cat 350 long-reach excavator.

Towards the end of the dredging job, on November 2, 2000, the *Panama* took on water through a cracked spud well during the early morning hours and rolled onto her side, dumping machinery, including a relatively new Cat excavator, to the bottom of the bay. Hanging on her side for several hours, the *Panama* finally turned over and sank, as pictured in this dramatic photo taken as the massive hull shows her bottom side while taking a dive to the bottom. Salvage crews worked to raise her until harsh winter conditions suspended the efforts until spring. Finally, on May 4, 2001, the *Panama* slowly rose to the surface while crews from Marine Tech's crane barge *B. Yetter* used gigantic pumps to force air into her tanks while dewatering the hull. The tug *Seneca* towed the barge into Fraser Shipyards for dry-docking and repair.

T-N-T Dredging's big hydraulic dredge, *Louise,* rests at Hallett Dock No. 7 in West Duluth. The giant leg extending out from her bow is lowered to the lakebed and the cutter head rotates, digging up the hard packed bottom while a huge Cooper Bessemer diesel powered pump sucks the mud up, like an enormous vacuum. The water drains out while the silt and mud (dredge spoils) are pumped either into scows or onshore through lengths of pipe that are, in some cases, thousands of feet long. On top of her control room are all the appropriate running lights and the "ball—diamond—ball" day shapes, signifying a vessel restricted in its ability to maneuver. In other words, if you see those shapes, do not expect that boat to move out of your way, he's not going anywhere. The *Louise* can be found dredging the small harbor of Ontonagon on Lake Superior's south shore for about one month each summer.

The last dipper dredge intact near the Great Lakes is the *DD-3*, as in "Dipper Dredge No. 3." Stored in the dry dock at Lyons, this state-owned dredge was used for dredging the Erie Canal to navigable depths. Powered by a steam hoist, this massive machine has a fold-down A-frame on the bow end. The dipper's leg and main stick are laid down on a utility scow that is faced up to the dredge while being towed. The smoke stack is disassembled and set on deck (a section of it can be seen at the corner of the superstructure). Her buckets rest on the stern and her spuds are pulled out and set on deck as well. Note that they are wooden spuds with steel framing. This old steamer is the last of the dinosaurs of the dredging industry. Today, cranes and clam buckets handle all mechanical dredging, working from Spud barges.

The New York State Department of Transportation has a well cared for fleet of commercial vessels designed for maintaining the Erie Canal. In addition to its active vessels, a few old timers remain in lay-up. Here, the *QB-10* sits in the Lyons dry dock. This quarters barge was once used for the crews bunkhouse on big dredging jobs along the canal system. The barge has many bunkrooms in addition to a lounge, galley, and large eating area. It is likely she will never sail again as quarters barges have become a thing of the past. With improved working conditions, crews are more likely to be put up in a motel during out of town jobs that would have once required the use of the *QB-10*.

On August 11, 1998 the big dipper dredge *Duluth* lifted her spuds for the last time. Although the fire in her boilers went out ten years earlier, her Caterpillar air compressor was pumping air to charge the system, enough to lift the spuds and the stick for one last tow, to the scrappers. Her history began in 1924 in Manitowoc, where the big wooden dipper dredge *No. 27* was built for the McMullen & Pitz Company. Sold to Zenith Dredge in 1945, the old leaky steamer worked hard until 1961 when she made her last dig. A newly constructed, welded steel hull was waiting in the Zenith yard when old *No. 27* was towed in for the last time. Her machinery was stripped, including everything from her bucket, deck winches, A-frame, and stick to the main hoist and boiler and placed on the new dredge, which was soon named *Duluth*, entering service in 1962. The hull, built by Fraser-Nelson and completed by Zenith Dredge, was placed under command of William Schroer and, 27 years later, made her last dig with Ronald North, only the second Captain to have command of the huge dredge. In 1999, she was gutted and reduced to a barge. Today, the remains of the famous old dipper are still sitting alongside the Duluth Timber Company's pier in Duluth.

—— Chapter 4: PASSENGERS——

In today's fast paced world, travel by passenger vessel is no more than a leisure activity for vacationers. Rather than a method of transportation between point A and point B, today's passenger vessels are now a place to relax, either on a weeklong cruise or a two-hour excursion ride. The passenger vessels are a place to gamble, a place to get a good meal, a place for live music and dancing, and a place to see the harbors and waterfronts from a unique vantage point.

The Great Lakes once supported dozens of large passenger steamships but are now left entirely without a regular passenger service, with the exception of short day runs. In the past, 75- to 200-foot passenger steamers visited the local harbors weekly and carried not only people but freight, livestock, and mail. Long-time residents in every area of the Great Lakes, with knowledge of their maritime past, will remember the vessels that served their area. Endless tales are told of the "packet" (package freighters) and passenger ships that served from port to port soon after the start of navigation and lasted into the 1950s.

Ferries are still popular on the Lakes. It is a long ride around Lake Michigan, through the always-heavy Chicago traffic or across the Upper Peninsula. The *Badger*, with her loyal following, keeps busy moving people and their vehicles on a 3½ hour boat ride across Lake Michigan between Manitowoc, Wisconsin and Ludington, Michigan. Local ferries, such as those running from Mackinaw City and St. Ignace to Mackinac Island, keep busy throughout the season, as do the Apostle Island ferries running to Madeline Island on Lake Superior and the ferries of Sandusky and Door County.

Smaller excursion vessels such as Diamond Jack's in Detroit and the Vista Fleet in Duluth give people the opportunity to view, up close, the harbor activity and visiting ships from the comfort of a safe, climate-controlled passenger boat. Just about every harbor around the Lakes now has one or two excursion vessels and some interesting areas of waterfront to tour. Excursion vessels are a fun way to sightsee in each harbor and view lighthouses, wrecks, scenic shoreline, and commercial operations with an unobstructed view.

From undeveloped film found on-board the bumboat *Kaner I*, this 1966 image shows the steamer *Ste. Claire* in her glory days, working on the Detroit River hauling passengers to the Bob-Lo Amusement Park. Built in 1910 by Toledo Shipbuilding, the 181-foot steamer is powered by a triple expansion steam engine with cylinder diameters of 20¾, 32, and 50¼ inches with a stroke of 36 inches. This beautiful steamer made her last run in September 1991 and laid up at the Nicholson Terminal in Detroit.

Up until their retirement, the Bob-Lo steamers *Columbia* and *Ste. Claire* were the last vessels in America where you could view one historic operating passenger steamboat from the deck of another. Built in 1902 at Wyandotte, the *Columbia* was the oldest working passenger steamer in the country during her last season of operation. A triple expansion engine built by Detroit Shipbuilding powers the 216 x 45-foot excursion vessel. She made her last run on September 2, 1991.

Through the years, since regular passenger service has ceased on the Lakes, several local and foreign operators have attempted to revive the tradition. Few were successful. In recent years, one such vessel, the *C. Columbus* broke that record by making several visits to the Lakes for many years in a row, with the vessel's maiden voyage to Duluth in 1997.

In addition to the local excursion vessels, a step up to the dinner boats gives passengers the same vantage point of the smaller tour boats but with some of the added luxury of the larger passenger ships. Dinner excursions tend to provide the passenger with a good meal and a chance to see their particular harbor or river during sunset and at night. Nighttime on the waterfront is usually a world that is peaceful, beautiful, and mesmerizing. Most dinner and excursion vessels are available for charter. Arrangements can be made to rent the entire vessel and its crew for group parties for special events or meetings.

While the old passenger steamers are now a distant memory for most of us, local passenger service, in the form of excursion boats and gambling ships, are still found in many ports across the Lakes. Interest in seeing the waterfront up close will always be with us, and the passenger boats, in one form or another, will live on.

Only eight years later, the *Ste. Claire* and her sister *Columbia* sit in a sad state of decay at Nicholson's, the same berth they laid up at in 1991. The *Columbia* was built by Detroit Shipbuilding Company as Hull No. 148 and has a slightly larger triple expansion engine than the *Ste. Claire*. The good news is the *Ste. Claire* has since been rescued from the boneyard and moved to Lorain where a full restoration is in progress. Studies are in progress on the feasibility of a restoration of the *Columbia* for the City of Detroit as well. At this point, these classic steamers have lasted far too long to be just thrown away. Those who are behind the restoration efforts deserve great applause.

The 65-foot passenger boat *Huron* was launched at Erie in 1955, built by Paasch Marine Services for the Arnold Lines at St. Ignace. Like many commercial vessels of her day, she was built with a 300-BHP Kahlenberg oil engine, which, in 1972, was replaced with an 8-cylinder Caterpillar D-379 diesel. That same year, the vessel was lengthened to 92 feet. She is still in service in the Straits of Mackinac, and is pictured here at St. Ignace on December 27, 1995, with a bow full of ice from the freezing spray that accumulates during her cold winter runs.

Passing Mackinac Island's famous Grand Hotel, the *Capt. Shepler* makes a run for Mackinaw City on October 22, 2001. Built by Aluminum Boats Incorporated at Crown Point, Louisiana, in 1986, this aluminum 900-HP passenger ferry is capable of making decent speeds across the Straits of Mackinac from Mackinaw City to St. Ignace. She is powered by twin V-12 71 Detroit diesels. Shepler's, Inc. owns the 78-foot long craft.

The Arnold Lines *Chippewa* is pictured here crossing the Straits on June 22, 2001. She is about to dock at St. Ignace for another load of passengers. Built by Paasch in 1962 at Erie, she was originally powered by a pair of Cat D-343s, which were replaced in 1989 with two Cummins KT-19m 450-HP diesels. The 65-foot vessel was taken back to Paasch during the 1964/1965 winter and lengthened to 85 feet.

The passenger steamer *Aquarama* sits idle at Buffalo in this 2000 photo. Built by Sun Shipbuilding & Dry Dock in Chester, Pennsylvania, on the Delaware River just below Philadelphia, the interesting looking vessel was launched in 1945 as the C4-S-B5 cargo ship *Marine Star*. Constructed for the U.S. Maritime Commission on a wartime contract, the *Star* was decommissioned after only a few years of service and sold to interests on the Great Lakes. Throughout 1955 and 1956, a conversion took place and soon after, the new 520-foot passenger vessel entered service on the Lakes. After operating only six years, the massive vessel went into lay-up at Muskegon in 1962, never to sail again. Since then, her new owners have towed her to various ports including Sarnia, Marysville, and Windsor, with big plans for the vessel, which have never materialized. Intact but in poor condition, the large turbine-powered ship is likely to make her next and final tow to a foreign ship breaking yard.

The passenger and auto ferry *Chi-Cheemaun* is in regular service between Tobermory, in the Bruce Peninsula and across to South Baymouth on Manitou Island. She was Hull No. 205 of the Collingwood Shipyards, built in 1974 for the Ontario Department of Highways. The 365-foot ferry makes for a fast, comfortable passage, saving a lot of driving time all the way around Georgian Bay. She is powered by two 16-cylinder Ruston-Paxman 3,500-HP diesels.

The *Badger* has made her place in history as the last coal fired ship on the Great Lakes. Between each trip, a dump truck drives into her car decks and dumps its load of coal into her bunkers. The *Badger* is also the last coal fired overnight passenger steamer in North America. She is in service between Manitowoc and Ludington on Lake Michigan and can save travelers a healthy amount of time going around the Lake, either through Chicago or the long route through the Upper Peninsula. The Christy Corporation constructed her at Sturgeon Bay for the Chesapeake & Ohio Railway in 1953. Measuring 410 feet long, the 8,000-HP ferry is powered by twin 4-cylinder steeple compound Skinner Uniflow steam engines.

The *Arthur K. Atkinson* was built in 1917 as the *Ann Arbor No. 6*, for the Ann Arbor Railroad. Service on Lake Michigan ended for this vessel in 1982 and two years later, the vessel was sold to Peterson Builders and towed to Kewaunee. Her triple expansion steam engine was removed during a 1959 rebuild, during which the vessel was given her present name, converted to diesel and repowered with a pair of 12-cylinder Nordberg engines. The vessel is shown here in lay-up at Ludington alongside the ferry *Spartan*. Shortly after this photo was taken, in 2003, the *Atkinson* was towed to Detour, at the lower end of the St. Mary's River. Now a controversial topic, the vessel is owned by a private party who intends to convert the ship into a floating plant for processing used tires into fuel oil.

Photographed in Menominee on August 6, 2003, the 1925 vintage car ferry *Viking I* sits at the K&K Warehousing dock, awaiting future work. Built as the *Ann Arbor No. 7* by Manitowoc Shipbuilding for the Ann Arbor Railroad, the vessel was given its present name in 1965 before being sold in 1975. Laid up in 1983 at Sturgeon Bay, the vessel was sold in 1993 for a proposed casino and underwent a major refit. On June 23, 1996, the vessel was towed to Port Stanley, Ontario. After the project failed, the ship was "repossessed" and departed under the cover of night, on an illegal crossing to Erie on October 24, 1996. After sitting there for many years with ongoing litigation, the vessel was finally sold to K&K in 2001 and towed there by the tug *Olive M. Moore*.

The small car ferry *C G Richter* was built in 1950 by Sturgeon Bay Ship-building & Dry Dock Company for Arni J. Richter of Washington Island, Wisconsin. The 70-footer is in service from Northport, Wisconsin in Door County to Washington Island. Originally powered by two Murphy 6-cylinder diesels (300 HP), the ferry was repowered in 1991 with a single 500-HP Cummins. Washington Island Ferry Line has operated the vessel since 1962. She is pictured on October 29, 1982. *Wendell Wilke photo*

The Madeline Island ferries run as late into the season as they possibly can. Here, the *Island Queen* departs Bayfield on January 17, 2001 for her crossing to LaPointe, on Madeline Island, part of the Apostle Islands. Built by Fraser Shipyards in 1966, the 80-foot ferry shuttles passengers and automobiles back and fourth until the ice becomes too thick, forcing a winter lay-up. During that period, wind sleds take over to get people to and from the Island. When the ice is thick enough, a highway is plowed and automobiles can drive across the lake.

Great Lakes shipyards, especially those in Sturgeon Bay and Marinette, have been known to construct a lot of hulls for off-Lakes use. In this September 2004 image at Marinette, the recently launched Staten Island ferry *Sen. John J. Marchi*, is undergoing completion of a few finishing touches before delivery to New York City under its own power. The giant double ender was built to replace an aging ferry fleet. This ferry is similar in design to the several generations of ferries before her that work around the New York City harbor. *Jon LaFontaine photo*

The 450-passenger liner *Polarlys* was built in 1952 in Denmark. Constructed for the Bergen Lines (BDB), the 270-foot vessel ran for them until January 1979 when it was transferred to Troms Flykes Dampski Bsselskab, which had taken over BDB's license in Hurtigruten that year. During her career, she collided with the Ofotens Steamship freighter *Stjernoy*, which sank in only five minutes. On February 27, 1972, she collided with another vessel at Maloysund, with only one life lost. Spending the remainder of the 1970s and 1980s in and out of retirement, the vessel was finally converted to a hospital ship in 1994 by Mercy Ships of Panama. Renamed *Caribbean Mercy*, she has made several visits to the Great Lakes and is a beautiful vessel, inside and out. She is pictured at the Duluth Entertainment and Convention Center dock during a June 1995 visit.

From time to time, someone attempts to start up a passenger operation on the Great Lakes, with a very slim success rate. Bad publicity from some health department inspections put an end to a short-lived cruise line on the Lakes. The 1968-built *Arcadia* was tied up in 2001, with violations in health and safety codes, which discouraged future passengers to the point of demanding refunds, leaving the ship with virtually no business. She was then tied up in Montreal, and left the Lakes on November 10, 2002 to be refurbished at Santiago de Cuba for Bahamian cruises. Not a bad ship, but a little bad publicity goes a long ways to damage business. Originally named *Vincente Puchol*, she was built as a Trans-Mediterranean ferry, but converted to a cruise ship in 1989. She is pictured here upbound in the Detroit River near Windsor on June 23, 2001.

Bound for Duluth, we pass the 1997-built ocean liner *C. Columbus* on her maiden voyage to the Great Lakes. Exchanging salutes, her friendly crew is justly proud to show off their new 476-foot vessel. Powered by Wartsila diesels, the shiny new vessel powers up as they head out across Lake Superior on October 4, 1997. This German passenger liner has made yearly visits to various Great Lakes ports. Before her arrival, it had been decades since any decent size passenger ships had run on the Lakes.

The *Cedar Point II* is virtually new in this photo, which was taken during her sea trials off Sandusky. Built in 1953 by Paasch Machine in Erie, the hull is nearly identical to those of the "Lake Erie style" fish tugs, but with open decks and a little more comfort for passengers. This 60-foot passenger vessel was in service at Sandusky until 2001. She had been renamed *Dispatch* in 1988 and received her current name of *Sawmill Explorer* in 1998. The vessel was built for the G. A. Boeckling Company of Sandusky and later worked for Cedar Point Transportation. *Authors collection*

Another excursion vessel with a fish tug design is the *Island Trader*, built by J. W. Nolan & Sons at Erie in 1952. Originally named *G. A. Boeckling II* and later *Cedar Point III*, the boat has worked out of Sandusky its entire life. Today, she is in service for the Cedar Point Transportation Company as the *Lady Kate*. The *Trader* is pictured at Sandusky in March 1997.

The small excursion vessel *Chippewa* is pictured at Perry Sound on March 15, 2000. Built as a Niagara Falls tour boat in 1955, she was originally named *Maid of the Mist III*, built by Russell Brothers. This attractive little passenger boat measures 60 x 16 x 6 feet.

Eglo Engineering Party built the beautiful yacht-like passenger vessel *Capt. Matthew Flinders* in 1984 at Port Adelaide, Australia. Measuring 144 x 40 x 8 feet, the vessel is powered by a Crossley model HRN-6 diesel, built in 1958. The ship runs from Toronto, operated by Mariposa Cruise Lines. She is pictured at Toronto on January 29, 1998.

The excursion vessel *Capt. Streeter* departs Chicago's Navy Pier on a foggy April 2002 afternoon. Built in 1987 at Salisbury, Maryland, she was originally named *M/V Chesapeake Shipbuilding 63*, named simply for her builder and the hull number. It is obvious that the vessel's construction order was cancelled or perhaps the boat was built as a demo. Shortly after her construction, she was sold to Shoreline Marine of Chicago and given her present name. The 65-foot vessel gives tours around the Chicago waterfront, working out of Navy Pier. Her fleetmate *Shoreline* can be seen returning in the background.

The *Vista Star* is photographed passing by the old forward superstructure off the steamer *Irvin L. Clymer* and the retired wooden fish tug *Last Chance*, both resting on the end of the Duluth Timber Company pier. The *Star* is part of the Vista Fleet's excursion boat fleet in the Twin Ports. Built in Freeport, Florida, as Hull No. 14 of the Freeport Shipbuilding & Marine Repair Company, she was launched in 1987 as the *Island Empress*. Bought the following year by the Vista Fleet, she was given her present name and put into service at Duluth, offering dinner cruises and harbor tours that provide a close-up view of the commercial docks and freighters.

The passenger vessel *Diamond Jack* passes upbound on August 18, 2001 with a load of sightseers. The Christy Corporation of Sturgeon Bay built her in 1955 as the *Emerald Isle* for Beaver Island Boat Company. After two decades with the Arnold Lines of Mackinac Island and a brief period in Milwaukee, Captain Bill Hoey purchased the vessel in 1991 for his Detroit River excursion line.

J. W. Nolan & Sons was a well-known boat builder at Erie. The 52-footer *Holiday* was one of their hulls, constructed in 1964 and currently working out of Cleveland. She is pictured outbound the Cuyahoga River on June 21, 2002. Although she serves as an excursion vessel, her design is much like a charter fishing vessel commonly found in the Southeast.

Chapter 5: FISH TUGS

One type of Great Lakes commercial vessel that is seeing great changes at the time of this writing is the fish tug. Commercial fishing was once a thriving industry on the Great Lakes but has slowly dwindled. Commercial fishing was one of the earliest industries on the Great Lakes. Large wooden sail and steam fish boats were put into service in the 1880s when fish stocks were undamaged. Anyone with a boat, or even seiners or pond-net fisherman, could go into the fishing industry and obtain huge catches. On the three upper lakes, Huron, Michigan, and Superior, lake trout was the premiere target, with whitefish close behind. Then came herring, chub, and perch, and later, smelt.

After the turn of the century, as the fish tug developed, gillnet fishing became popular along with seining and hook rigs. The industry grew and during WWII, many of the old steam and sailing vessels were replaced with modern steel and wooden gas or diesel tugs. During this time, production was crucial and fish prices were high.

In the early years of the industry, the need for bigger boats caused many fishermen to begin using old harbor tugs. Tugs originally built for towing or logging operations, even packet boats engaged in freight and passenger service, could also be employed, now and again, for lifting nets.

Unemployed harbor tugs could be leased to the fishermen who, in turn, installed temporary enclosures on the bow to protect them from the harsh weather. Net lifters were installed on the side of the bow where they can still be found. Eventually, additional enclosures were made, protecting the stern, where their catch could be stored until they reached port. In due course, older tugs were purchased and enclosed entirely. With that, the root of the name "fish tug" is obvious. Throughout history, the hulls of fishing vessels have closely resembled that of tugboats. Quite often, their duties would blend, with not only tugboats being converted to fish tugs, but later fishing tugs being converted into towing tugs.

The methods of fishing have changed throughout the years and continue to change. On the upper lakes, the majority of the tugs built were for gillnet fishing. Gillnets are long lengths, up to two miles, of netting that are set on the lake bottom. The main objection to gillnets is that they are not selective. Fish die when they are gilled, providing no opportunity to return unwanted fish to the lake. However, for an experienced gillnet fisherman, selection of mesh size, water depth and bottom conditions can accurately capture its targeted species and smaller fish can swim through while larger fish can bounce off the mesh.

Trapnet tugs have an entirely different look altogether. With a small cabin on the extreme forward end and a large open work deck, these boats have

One of many designed by the Burger Boat Company of Manitowoc, the 52-foot steel tug *Ida S.* is pictured at Milwaukee in September 2002. Built with a 100-120 Kahlenberg diesel, she was constructed in 1948 for the Seger Fish Company of Sheboygan. Later converted to a trawler, she was converted back to a gill net tug after only a few years in the 1960s. Now owned by Philip Anderson Fisheries of Kewaunee, the tug is on its third engine, a 300-HP Volvo diesel, which had replaced a 270-HP Cummins.

This is an early tugboat in winter service as a fish tug, modified with a temporary enclosure over the stern. In this rare image, the tug is pictured without her bow enclosure, but fishing equipment is visible on her forward deck. Heading out in a rough Lake Michigan sea, the *Eagle* is a tough 50-foot steamer built in 1905 in Wisconsin. An eagle mascot can be seen bolted to her pilot-house roof, an old tradition on many tugs from that era.

ample room to stack traps and buoys. To some fishery managers, trapnets are the preferred entrapment gear. Fish captured in trapnets can be sorted by species and size and undesirables can be returned to the lake, unharmed.

As the heyday of commercial fishing drew to an end, issues such as over-fishing, pollution, and invasive species became the talk of the industry. By the 1950s, the depletion of fish stocks became an increasing concern. The great demand for fish during WWII and the high market prices pushed fisherman to invest in more gear and man hours, bringing in greater catches, which in turn, contributed to pushing certain species, such as lake trout, toward extinction.

Pollution, again from the mass productions of WWII and earlier, greatly contributed to the demise of fish populations. Pollution control was, at the time, not particularly important. Contaminants introduced to the air and waters of the Great Lakes were (for the most part) not known to be harmful. The Great Lakes are noted to be extremely clean today, but there is no doubt that old industries, such as logging and mining, greatly contributed to the damage of fish population.

With the opening of the St. Lawrence Seaway, invasive species, brought in through ocean going ships'

ballast water, have greatly affected the fish stocks in the Great Lakes. Sea lamprey was the number one culprit in the premature death of lake trout stocks. Lake Huron was affected first, then Lake Michigan, and finally Lake Superior was nearly ruined by the mid-1960s. At that time, trout fishing was closed off on the Lakes, destroying what had once been the backbone of the industry.

With the good years of commercial fishing nearing the end, government buyouts of the fishermen's licenses followed. With most Great Lakes commercial fishing on the U.S. side left only to tribal fishermen, the bulk of the fishing fleets have been put into the boneyards at marinas and shanty villages around the Lakes. As waterfront property becomes more valuable, the old fishing shanties are bulldozed and the tugs go with them.

Today, we are at the end of an era for most commercial fishing on the Great Lakes. The days of the family fishing business are nearly gone. It is rare to see a fishing shanty in someone's backyard with the old wooden tug ready to work. The colorful display of buoys, flags, and net racks along the shores of our Lakes are hard to find. Even the boneyards are thinning, with the old tugs being bulldozed or cut up for scrap. One of the industries that first brought settlers to these shores is all but gone.

The *Donna I* is a WWII era Canadian tug with the center pilothouse, standard design for the big Lake Erie tugs. Tucked away in the small village of Hurkett, Ontario, the *Donna* is a time capsule that shows every detail of her era, including detailed interior woodwork, classic 1945 lines, and a vintage Gray Marine diesel. This 55-footer remains in limited service along with another classic, *F. T. James*. The Northern Marine & Engine Company of Bronte, Ontario, built both tugs during the same year.

Looking a little rough but still hard at work, the 1946 wooden tug *Donna Belle* is laying out near the ferry docks as winter approaches in Bayfield. Smoke from her stovepipe indicates a warm cozy environment inside this Apostle Islands workhorse on a cold November day. Originally named *Lily May* and built by Frank Muhlke, she was powered by a Gray Marine gas engine but later repowered by a Detroit 6-71 diesel. The vessel has since had steel plating placed over her wood hull, a process often referred to as "bustling."

Another Bayfield builder was Evan Christensen, who built the 28-foot wooden tug *Bobbie* in 1939. Powered by a 2-cylinder Regal 18-HP gas engine, the gillnet tug was built for William Noring and fished from Sand Island. Later repowered with a 115-HP Chrysler Crown gas engine, the tug was sold to Louis Peterson of Bayfield, of who's nickname the tug recieved years later: *Uncle Butts*. Typical of many old Lake Superior tugs, she had thin steel plate over her rotting wooden hull, plywood cabins, and homemade portholes after years of modifications and tar and shingle roofing. Pulled up at Bayfield since at least the 1990s, the *Butts* will likely never sail again.

The *John R.* has spent the last decade pulled ashore in a small area of Bayfield that has become a natural boneyard for fish tugs. Many have "wintered" there, never to see service again. The wooden 32-footer was built by Frank Muhlke, a well-known boat builder who constructed many fish tugs in Bayfield. Originally the *Flo*, she later became *Mar-Jean* and finally *Susan K.* before being given her present name.

Launched as the *Apostle Islands*, the Kahlenberg-powered package freighter was built by Burger Boat for Booth Fisheries of Bayfield. The 55-footer was used to pick up fish from the Apostle Island fisheries, delivering them to market and also to run supplies, mail and passengers to the Islands. She would be equipped with a net lifter for the Fall herring runs. In 1959, the vessel was sold to Sivertson Fisheries of Superior and renamed *Hiawatha*. This converted fish tug maintained her original 1938 configuration and because of her appearance, she is commonly mistaken for a former bumboat, sharing a design similar to the large Kaner family bumboats of Duluth. After several years of inactivity, she was sold in 1997 for private use. In December of that year, her stern cabin was cut away to make an open deck. That winter, the entire superstructure was cut in half, horizontally, and raised about one foot, providing more head room inside. Her Kahlenberg was removed and a Detroit 6-71 put in its place. The vessel currently acts as a boat brokerage office in Duluth.

Beautiful lines indeed, the unique design of this 42-foot, 1937 Sturgeon Bay Shipbuilding hull is shown in profile. Photographed in 1999, Desjarden's tug *Shelly* sits at her Manistique pier. Built with a 75-90 Kahlenberg engine, she was repowered in the 1970s with a Volvo diesel. The tug was built for the DeVet family of Fayette, who owned it until 1974. The tug remains in service today, working out of Manistique.

The sleek, wooden 40-footer *Twin Disc* is another tug that has had steel plating installed over her hull, giving it strength for ice breaking and protecting its aging wood planking. Built in 1937 by Peterson Boat Works at Sturgeon Bay, this tug was ordered by the Twin Disc Clutch Company to demonstrate marine reduction gears. After only a couple of years, the vessel was sold and went into fishing service. During that time, the race was on to build power that is more efficient for boats, replacing large, heavy steam engines and direct reversing oil engines. After many years, the Twin Disc Company did become one of the premier makers of marine transmissions and these are a common sight in commercial boats today. The *Twin Disc* cuts a nice wake in this early morning photo as she leaves the Wisconsin mainland for the Apostle Islands and eventually Lake Superior to pull nets.

Shark jaws have been known to show up on more than one fish tug over the years. Here, the *Doughboy Jr.* is pictured in June 2003 at her home pier at the Lower Entry of the Keweenaw Waterway in Michigan. Launched by Marinette Marine in 1947, the 40-footer was built with a Cat D-318 diesel and later repowered with another engine of the same type. Originally working out of Waukegan, the tug later fished from Fayette and Fairport until being purchased by her current owners in 1985. The original wooden tug *Doughboy*, coincidently, also worked from the Keweenaw and can still be seen today, abandoned only a half mile from where the *Jr.* docks.

The interior of a typical stern pilothouse gillnet tug. This one, the 1945 Burger hull *Trio*, is a 36-footer that worked for Emil Pagel out of Algoma since she was built until the 1980s. After a time in Portage, the tug was trucked to Port Wing on Lake Superior where Russell Bailey fished it for a decade until it was sold to VonRiedel Marine Services in 1998. Two years later, it was sold to Peterson Fisheries and trucked to Muskegon where the old wooden superstructure visible in this photo was replaced with new steel. Her 6-cylinder 6-121 Gray Marine gas engine was replaced with a Cummins diesel. To the left, is her auxiliary control station with wheel and throttle, which allowed the tug to be operated from the side,

where the nets are being lifted. Next is the shiny guide roller, which swings out over the side once her doors are open. Nets are pulled over this device by the big round "net lifter" which is in the center. The hydraulically operated winch turns slowly with teeth that open and close, pulling the net in and releasing it on the other side as the crew pulls the fish out onto the wooden tables just after the lifter.

One of the better-known fish tugs on the Lakes is the 1937-vintage 40-footer *Linda E.* built by Burger Boat at Manitowoc. She was originally powered by a 50-60 Kahlenberg oil engine and owned by LeClair Fisheries of Two Rivers. In 1960, the vessel was sold to Leif Weborg of Milwaukee and, soon after, repowered with a Cummins diesel. On a beautiful, clear, calm day the tug and its experienced three-man crew were bound for Port Washington with 1,000-pounds of chub. They had phoned in, giving an update on their ETA, situated 9 miles southeast of port and 6 miles offshore. The tug never arrived. On December 11, 1998, the well-maintained *Linda E.* vanished without a

trace. She left no signs of sinking, no debris, no oil slick, and she took the entire crew with her. After years of searching and ongoing investigations, the vessel was finally located in 260 feet of water on June 18, 2000 by the Navy minesweeper USS *Defender*. The vessel was found to have extensive damage to her starboard side. At the time of this writing, speculation is that she was rammed by a large tank barge and sank in a matter of seconds, too fast for any reaction by the crew of either vessel, both of which may not have even known what happened. The tug is photographed here at her Milwaukee home pier on December 28, 1995.

The Bayfield tug *Oral* is pulled ashore for repairs in this July 2003 image. This sleek-looking 38-footer is powered by a Detroit 6-71 diesel, which had replaced an old Cat, and before that, a 30-36 Kahlenberg oil engine. Built by and for Peterson Fisheries of Muskegon in 1955, the vessel was sold in 1975 to Brimley, Michigan, and later ended up in Michigan City before being trucked to Bayfield in 1998 for her current owner Mark Montano.

A gill-netter with an old appearance, but a modern design is the classy *Pep*, working out of Marinette in this 1999 photo. Her roller for the net lifter can be seen sticking out of the bow doorway. These are to guide the nets smoothly over the side and into the tug. The *Pep* is working from the very port where Marinette Marine built her in 1971. Nice and beamy, she measures in at 42 feet long and 18 feet wide, with a 6-foot draft. In the background, the ocean going ship *Federal Oslo* is offloading steel ingots.

One of the biggest tugs working in the Apostle Island area is Newaygo's *Thomas C. Mullen*, built by Burger Boat in 1946. At 48 feet long, this center-house gillnet tug was yet another built with a Kahlenberg oil engine, but repowered in 1957 with a Detroit 6-71. The tug was originally built for Robert Ludwig of Michigan City and was sold in 1957 when it was converted to a trawler, working out of the Saugatuck area. Around 1980, it came to Bayfield and was converted back to a gillnet tug. She is pictured here at her home pier, with the *Wolverine II, RVH,* and *Oral* in the background.

Another design is the fully enclosed forward pilothouse tug, more common on the Canadian side. This one, the *Pilgrim*, launched as the *Verlyn* in 1946 at Vermilion, Ohio, shows little of her original appearance, having undergone more than one rebuild over the years. The tug has seen multiple owners and worked in ports including Toledo, Lorain, Buffalo, Grand Island, Conneaut, and now Erie, where she was photographed in July 2002. *Al Hart photo*

The G-tug *Maine*? No. Well, maybe briefly, for the movie *VI Warshawkski*, which was filmed in Chicago. Painted in G-tug colors, unofficially renamed *Maine* and blown up in the movie, this poor old tug has laid around on the Calumet River ever since. With her large C-model Kahlenberg, this tug was built as the fish tug *Stamina* in 1931. Fishing for only a few years, the hull was sold in 1936 and converted to a towing tug. Renamed *Grand Haven* in 1968, Bultema Dredge & Dock Company of Muskegon had purchased the tug the year before. Admittedly an odd looking vessel, it is easy to wonder what she looked like when still working as a fish tug, some 70 years ago.

The towing tugs *Tolsma Bay* and *Callie M.* were, coincidentally, both built as 65-foot fish tugs in 1910 on Lake Erie. They may be the only two tugs on the Lakes with that claim to fame; they pose in Duluth purposefully in this rare October 2003 photograph. Originally named *Willard L.*, the *Tolsma* worked for 20 years for the Case Fish Company of Cleveland before being converted to a towing tug. *Callie* held out a little longer, fishing until 1945 when the Zenith Dredge Company of Duluth converted it to a towing tug. Her original name of *Chattanooga* was kept until 1979.

The *Beverly R. Goodison*, of 1938 is a classic Canadian "Lake Erie style" fish tug. This 65-footer was sold into U.S. ownership in 1994 after spending a lifetime working out of Port Dover, one of the largest fishing ports on Lake Erie. Unable to work commercially in the U.S., thanks to the Jones Act, the tug was used very little and sat in Cheboygan, where it is seen in this March 1999 photo sporting a "For Sale" sign taped to her cabin. In 2002, the vessel was donated to the Sea Scouts of Michigan City. The tug has a steel hull and aluminum superstructure, which was added during a rebuild in the 1970s. She is powered by a 300-HP Detroit 8-71 diesel.

A fine example of a typical Canadian fish tug is the 1971 *Mi-Mar-Lynne*, owned by Lynn-Dover Foods. These long, fat, steel hulled boats are tremendously stout tugs, built for their unique Great Lakes service. This 95-gross ton, 70-footer is pictured in June 2004 at Port Stanley, a large fishing port on the Canadian side of Lake Erie. In port that day were 18 large fish tugs and every one of them active.

The *Leonard S.* is a rather large and unique Canadian fish tug, photographed at Port Dover in March 2003. This 80-footer was built in 1979. With a 30-foot beam, this heavy-duty tug is one that is built to take on some serious weather. Visible in the photo, toward the back, are two black cones with their apexes together, which identifies a vessel engaged in fishing.

Photographed ashore at Naubinway in 1999, the trap net tug *Lauris C.* is a spare boat now. She was launched 40 years earlier, built by the T. D. Vinette Company of Escanaba. The 40-footer was originally a fully enclosed gillnet tug built for Christensen Brothers of Marquette. Her original Buda diesel was later replaced with a Cummins and today is powered by a V-8 Perkins. The tug was converted to a trap net tug, with the construction of a small forward pilothouse. The removal of her entire cabin created a large open deck, giving ample room for equipment.

The Toledo-built trap net tug *Max B.* has just arrived at its home dock in Munising on June 26, 2004 and her cargo is being offloaded. These types of tugs are, for the most part, all open deck with square sterns with space to stack the fish traps and provide easy access to the water from any position on the boat. Built in 1958 for the Vino Fish Company of Curtice, Ohio, the 34-foot tug is now owned by Our Sons Fisheries of Munising.

Returning to her home pier, the *Wolverine II* turns into her slip at Bayfield. The 39-foot steel Burger hull was built in 1940 with a Hill Diesel; it was later replaced by a Detroit 4-71. Originally a Lake Michigan boat, the tug came to Lake Superior in the 1950s, working from the Portage Entry in the Keweenaw peninsula. It is obvious by this photo that operating a fish tug is like driving a tank: extremely limited visibility. The operators are highly skilled captains, true sailors, often with many decades of experience. Later repowered with a Detroit 6-71, this 250-HP diesel tug is still in regular service.

The tug *Judy* lifts nets on June 20, 2003 off the south shore of Lake Superior. Anxious seagulls wait for their dinner as the fish are cleaned and packed in crates aboard the tug. Local fish markets usually have the fish within hours of the fresh lift. The *Judy* is another Marinette Marine hull, built in 1954, measuring 34 feet long by 11 feet 6 inches wide. She came from Copper Harbor to Port Wing, Wisconsin, where she is still in service.

Originally named Edith J., this 52 x 14 foot tug was built in 1945 by Burger Boat Co. After service for the Jones Fish Co. of Ontonagon, Michigan it was purchased in 1955 by Lawrence Schweig of Chicago. Everett Johnson worked for Schweig, and eventually purchased the tug which he renamed *Julie Ann* in 1974. She is still in service, having been repowered with a Cummins diesel. She is shown here returning to the harbor at Port Wing, Wisconsin with a fresh catch in July 2004. *Deena Neumann Photo*

Chapter 6: WORKBOATS

The term "workboat" can be applied to nearly any vessel performing commercial tasks. In addition to those covered in previous chapters, dozens more can be found around the Great Lakes. These vessels are often designed for multiple duties and are often bought, sold, and converted for use in other areas.

Self-propelled dredges were once a common sight on the Lakes, particularly Lake Erie, on both the Canadian and U.S. shores. They carefully remove clean sand from the lakebed for use in the construction trade. These "sandsuckers" are similar to hydraulic dredges, although they carry their cargo onboard, in cargo holds, rather than pumping it to a disposal site. Unlike dredges, sandsuckers' product is valuable and is delivered to a dock for unloading and processing.

Small workboats, usually less than 40 feet in length, can be found in nearly every port on the Lakes. They are used for dock repairs, dive work, surveying, and tending construction jobs, among other things. These handy little steel craft are there to make a buck for their owners, either on a steady basis or a few times throughout the year, as needed.

Research and survey vessels can be found working throughout the Lakes for the local colleges or government entities including the U.S. Geological Survey, U.S. Army Corps of Engineers, or the Environmental Protection Agency. These vessels are used for surveying depths, sediments, pollution, fish populations, and all other areas of environmental concern. Scientists from around the world come to the Great Lakes to engage in studies from the laboratories onboard these vessels.

The large Lakeboats and ocean-going vessels are in need of services while visiting the ports. Less common today, fuel and supplies were always delivered to these boats in smaller vessels. A few remain today, including fuel tankers such as Gaelic's bunkering barge *Marysville* in Detroit and Hannah's *William L. Warner* working from the Indiana Harbor area.

The mail boat *J. W. Westcott II* can be found delivering mail to those ships transiting the Detroit River. While underway, the *Westcott* pulls alongside the larger vessel and mail is exchanged via a bucket. Crews can also change using the mail boat or pilot boats around the Lakes.

The *Incan Superior* was a famous vessel to those living in the Twin Ports or on the North Shore of Lake Superior who were able to watch her pass, usually twice daily. Built in 1974 at North Vancouver, the 373-foot long railcar ferry was used to shuttle train cars from Thunder Bay, Ontario across the Lake to Superior, Wisconsin. The ship backed into a dock where a "ramp" was connected to the ship. Rails led right out onto the ship and switch engines of the Burlington Northern in Superior used a string of several empty flat cars as a "stick" to push the train cars onto the vessel, thus keeping the weight of the heavy locomotives away from the edge of the dock. Often referred to as "the paper boat" because of its common cargo of pulp products, the *Incan* was one of the fastest ships operating on the Lake. For those living along the shore, she was easily recognized by her distinct sound. Service discontinued at the end of the 1992 season, sadly ending an 18-year tradition. Today, she is in operation out of Vancouver under the name *Princess Superior*.

Another former U.S. Navy landing craft sold into civilian use is the *Columbus*, which began life as *LST-987* in 1944 at the yards of the Boston Naval Yard. The 328-foot long vessel was converted to a sand dredge in 1973. She is pictured underway in Lake Erie in July of 1995. As her sand cargo is pumped in and settles in her hold, the lake water is discharged. As an LST, she served on the East Coast of the United States and saw limited wartime service. After decommissioning, the vessel was to be sold to the German Navy, a deal that fell through and the ship was instead sold for conversion to a sand dredge in Panama. Her service began on the Great Lakes in 1978 and she has worked periodically, mostly on Lake Erie, under the names *Esperance III* and since 1986, *Columbus. Al Hart Photo*

Chandler boats bring supplies that are ordered by the vessel owners. These days, most docks are accessible by road and these delivery boats have slowly disappeared, since it is easier to deliver the supplies with a van. Delivery by vehicle eliminates the liabilities and maintenance of a vessel, not to mention avoiding the dangers of foul weather in the harbors.

In the busy ports around the Lakes, bumboats were once a common sight. These small peddler's boats were out to sell goods or services directly to the sailors on visiting ships. The Kaner family of the Twin Ports invented the Great Lakes bumboat service. Several brothers and cousins began peddling goods at the train stations and soon expanded their route with bicycles to include the docks. With business so lucrative at the harbor, a small wooden vessel was eventually purchased and converted to the Lake's first bumboat. Having an English root, the term "bumboat" was applied by sailors who, in their ocean travels, knew of similar vessels that would bring prostitutes out to incoming ships.

Business grew in the Twin Ports harbor and word spread. Eventually, bumboats began popping up all over the Lakes. The first custom-built steel bumboat

was constructed for the Kaner family in 1934 and several followed, each one bigger and better until the last one, which was built in 1959. The 1960s were the end of an era for bumboats, as their numbers slowly dwindled. The zero-tolerance alcohol policies aboard steamships of the late 1980s spelled the end of the bumboats, which did most of their business as floating bars.

Another service greatly needed by the steamships of the Lakes is ice breaking. While ice breaking and dock clearing in each port is left up to the commercial tugboat companies, maintenance of critical waterways is the responsibility of the U.S. Coast Guard. Coast Guard cutters maintain waterways such as St. Mary's River, the Straits of Mackinac, and the St. Clair River. These heavily built icebreakers can cut through several feet of ice, ice that most tugboats cannot penetrate. Coast Guard cutters will also be called out into the harbors when ice conditions are deemed too intense for the local harbor tugs.

The support craft covered in this general category play a vital roll in the harbor operations and of larger vessels working on the Lakes.

YO-178 was built by Smith's at Pensacola in 1945 on a WWII contract. This 175-foot tanker was a Yard Oiler, designated "YO" by the U.S. Navy. They were used for moving oil in the coastal trade and more commonly, bunkering ships. Of the hundreds of YO tankers built, only a few remain. In this image, the tanker has already been renamed *Lake Edward* under civilian ownership and is pictured at the Erie Sand dock in June 1967 undergoing a conversion to a sandsucker. *Author's collection*

This is the former *YO-178* as she looks today. The sandsucker *J. S. St. John*, of the Erie Sand Company, unloads at their home dock in Erie on April 18, 2001. Her original 6-cylinder 14 x 19-inch bore and stroke Union diesel was replaced with an 8-cylinder 645 EMD during the 1967 rebuild. In this photo, her suction leg can be seen on the starboard side, mostly submerged, but rising towards the stern. The vessel is sitting deep in the water with a full load of lake sand, about to be unloaded by the company's Mantiowoc crane.

Laying at the Sandusky Erie Sand terminal on March 16, 1997 is the vulnerable old sandsucker *John R. Emery*, a name she has worn since 1925. Built by William J. Kingston in 1905 at Buffalo, the self-unloading freighter was originally named *Trenton*. It is difficult to imagine in this age of 1,000-footers, but this 140-foot hull was once a decent sized freighter. Converted to a sandsucker in 1925, this old steamship once looked like a "mini-*Richard Reiss*." She had forward cabins and A-frame with a self-unloader and a tall steam smoke stack. Converted to diesel in 1958 and her cabins reconfigured, her pilothouse now sits aft and her forecastle now holds a massive diesel powered pump for sucking sand. This floating vacuum cleaner has a large leg that is lowered down to the bottom of the lake (visible down the starboard side) and sucks the nice clean lake sand up and into her holds. The sand is dumped ashore and used in various applications for which clean, washed, filtered sand is needed.

The *James M. Bray* is photographed on June 18, 1997 as she motors back into the Corps of Engineers dock at Sault Ste. Marie. As modern as this self-propelled hydrographic survey vessel may look, it was actually built in 1924 as a deck barge. The *Bray* was built by the Sturgeon Bay Shipbuilding & Dry Dock Company for the Corps and originally named *Deck Cargo Barge 20*. The 128-foot vessel was converted in 1985 and given a pair of Detroit 6v-92TA diesels for propulsion. The unit is based at Sault Ste. Marie, Michigan.

The Hans Hansen Welding Company built the Port Huron pilot boat, *Huron Maid*, at Toledo in 1977. This 42-foot workboat is typical of a fleet of vessels used in nearly every port in the United States where pilots are used. Local pilots are brought out on pilot boats to visiting ships with crews who are unfamiliar with the rivers and harbors. The pilot acts as Captain, or guide, on the vessel while transiting in his territory. In the ocean ports, special docking pilots supplied by the tugboat companies often dock the ship once it has arrived in port.

The Detour pilot boat *Linda Jean* began life as a gillnet tug. Arnold Johnson built the steel fish tug at Green Bay in 1950. In 1974, it was sold to Seaway Services Corporation and converted to a pilot boat.

Fuel is often delivered to the visiting ships by small tankers or tank barges. In this photo taken at the Duluth ore docks, the small tanker *William H. Bennett* is bunkering oil on the steamer *Arthur M. Anderson*. Essentially a 90-foot self-propelled barge, the *Bennett* was built by Blount Industries in Warren, Rhode Island, in 1950 for West Shore Fuel of Buffalo. They ran it for ten years before selling it to Marine Fueling of Cleveland, which operated the boat in Duluth. She was only Hull No. 4 at Blount, which has since become one of the major builders of workboats in the U.S. The vessel was sold in 1982 to East Coast interests but never re-documented. Disposition of the vessel is unknown.

In this 1998 image taken at Toledo, Gaelic's tug *Shannon* has the fuel barge *Marysville* in tow. Crews are fueling the steamer *John J. Boland* while it is unloading. The tanker *Marysville* was built in St. Louis, Missouri, in 1973 and is a double-hull petroleum barge used for bunkering ships.

At the DM&IR No. 6 ore dock in Duluth, the tanker *Reiss Marine* slowly pushes through the ice, ready to bunker the steamer *Reserve*, which is loading taconite pellets. Built in Warren, Rhode Island, by Blount Industries in 1978, the 160-foot tanker served the Duluth harbor for 20 years fueling ships; she replaced the aging bunkering tanker *William H. Bennett*, also built by Blount. The vessels now have to stop at the Port Terminal to take on bunkers from Murphy Oil. The *Reiss Marine* saved each ship at least a couple of hours by delivering the fuel to them while they were loading. Apparently not profitable in today's market, the *Reiss Marine* was sold in recent years to Hispanic interests and left the Lakes. She is powered by a pair of 12v-149 Detroit diesels.

The steamer *Kaye E. Barker* is moored at the Duluth Port Terminal docks waiting for her turn to load. A lot is happening on this dreary, cold Duluth day. Tied alongside is the fueling tanker *Reiss Marine*, which is pumping bunker fuel onto the ship. An all-red fueling flag can be seen flying on the tanker. On the dock, trucks from Northern Engineering are on hand while repair crews assist with engine room mechanical issues. The bright yellow step van owned by Eugene Kolstad is parked near the gangway. This "bumbus," as it was known, was the rubber-tired version of the bumboat, and was commonly found parked alongside every ship in port for a few hours at a time since the 1980s, until Kolstad passed away in 2003.

In Cleveland on July 27, 1984, the bumboat *Forest City* lays along a Steinbrenner steamship and is open for business. The *Forest City* lays claim to the first ever custom built bumboat on the Great Lakes. Designed and built in Superior by Louis Dahlgren, she was launched stern first into the Hughitt Slip in 1934. Built with twin stacks, this 47-foot heavily built, riveted hull served originally for the Kaner family and was named the *Kaner Bros.* She worked the Duluth harbor for 43 years before being sold to Captain Gregory Rudnick of Cleveland who changed her name to *Forest City*. He operated the vessel from 1977 into the 1980s as the last bumboat on the Cuyahoga River. The boat was briefly and unofficially renamed *Abe Kaner* while in operation at Allouez during the late 1960s. The *Kaner Bros.* was the model for the larger *Marine Trader*, built for the Kaner family five years later. On February 27, 1999, Abraham Kaner passed away at age 91. He was the last of the brothers who developed the Great Lakes bumboat concept.*Al Hart photo*

The bumboat *Sonny II* is outbound in the port of Ashtabula on September 24, 1992. She was the last bumboat operating on Lake Erie and can still be found there, engaged in a similar trade amongst recreational boats. The Harbor Supply Company has owned the 40-foot vessel since its construction in 1959. The Lake Shore Boiler & Welding Company at Ashtabula built her. Bumboats each had their own unique look to them. Not the prettiest boats on the Lakes, but they were built to serve a unique purpose and their design maximized the use of its interior space to store and display goods. While the *Sonny II* was like other bumboats in most respects, she was unique in that when not doing business with the ships, she could be found up river, open for business with the pleasure boaters. *Al Hart photo*

One of the more famous bumboats in Duluth was the *Kaner I*, built in 1950 as the *Ted* for Ted Gozanski of Superior. Built by Marks Welding at Vermilion, the *Ted* was the last of three nearly identical bumboats built in consecutive years for service at Duluth. Upon delivery to the port, a trade was made with the Kaner family for their 1948-built boat *Kaner*. The *Ted* was immediately renamed *Kaner I* and placed into service at Duluth, covering the coal and ore docks, even after all the other bumboats had gone out of business. One of the more famous vessels on the Lakes, the bright orange bumboat was a regular caller to all the boats visiting the Twin Ports harbor in the 1980s and 1990s. The *Kaner I* is pictured alongside the 1,000-footer *Oglebay Norton* during one of its last days of operation.

In 1998, VonRiedel Marine Services, which operated the *Marine Trader*, purchased the *Kaner I* in order to keep it out of the hands of competitors. Originally powered by a 6-cylinder Universal-Nordberg gas engine, in 1998 the retired bumboat was given the 6-71 diesel from the fish tug *Nels J.* Today the bumboat is privately owned and is not in commercial service. Bernard Kaner was the last one to operate the vessel as a bumboat. Renamed *Marine Supplier*, the boat is shown here in May 2001, between paint schemes at the Northern Pacific ore dock in Allouez. These "Vermilion hulls" proved to be quite successful as bumboats, with square sterns that gave them increased cargo capacity.

Many assumed Bernie's retirement of the *Kaner I* spelled the end of the bumboats in Duluth. Four years later, the *Marine Trader* was fitted out once more, reviving a tradition that had begun 80 years earlier. Built in 1939 by National Iron in Duluth, the *Trader* was the biggest bumboat ever on the Great Lakes. In 1952, she was lengthened to 65 feet, exceeding her own record by 9 feet. Operated by "Honest Al" Kaner until his death in 1986, the boat went into lay-up at Duluth's Lakehead Boat Basin. Purchased by VonRiedel Marine in 1995, the vessel underwent a two-year overhaul before returning to service as the last bumboat in North America. Built with a heavy riveted hull, the *Trader* was known to be a good icebreaker and ran late into the season every year. The vessel served most of her life at the Allouez ore docks. Laid up once again in 2000, she is now facing an uncertain future. She is pictured alongside the Great Lakes Fleet steamer *John G. Munson* at the DM&IR ore dock on May 31, 1998.

The bumboat *Marine Trader* pulls up at the Allouez ore docks on July 22, 1995, behind the 1,000-footer *Burns Harbor*. Due to the height of modern ships, the bumboats would often tie up at the dock, behind the ship so that sailors could see they were open for business. In this photo, the bumboat is out on sea trials after being placed back in the water for the first time in eight years.

In 1999, the *Trader* is moored alongside the Paterson Steamship Company freighter *Paterson,* which is loading grain at AGP in Duluth. The ship's crew has come aboard to pick up a few supplies and souvenirs from the port. Note the massive amount of inventory jammed into a tight space on the 65-foot vessel.

Crewmembers off the ships were pleased with the layout of the *Trader* and her bright, friendly atmosphere. Bumboats of old had always been known to be a little on the dark and messy side. Glass display cases hold knives, models, jewelry, nautical gifts, belt buckles, and lighters. Along the wall are all the medicines and toiletry items. On the counters are more souvenir type items, ship photos and of course, some tunes are playing on the boombox. The register is up front with soda coolers below. All of the tobacco products, including cigars, cigarettes, and pipe tobacco, are on the back wall. The exit is upstairs through the pilothouse. Her large wooden wheel and brass controls can be seen up front.

Warming up for another run, the *Trader* sits at the Duluth Timber dock on November 28, 1999. Her perfect reflection on the water shows what a beautiful night it is for a boat ride in the Twin Ports harbor. The time is 20:30 and after a 10-minute trip, the *Trader* could be found tied alongside its customer, the Canadian steamship *Montrealais* at the Cargill B-1 elevator.

Often mistaken for bumboats, other supply boats serve the ships of the Great Lakes, delivering provisions paid for by the steamship companies. While the bumboats are out peddling goods directly to the sailors, the supply and chandler boats deliver engine parts, galley stores, and supplies ordered in advance. The *Ojibway* was built in 1946 as Hull No. 526 at the Great Lakes Engineering Works in Ashtabula. The vessel has operated from the Soo Warehouse at Sault Ste. Marine its whole life. Built for and operated by the U.S. Steel fleet, the vessel was sold in recent years and is now operated by MCM Marine, owners of the Sault Ste. Marine shipyard and dry dock. The *Ojibway* is pictured in October 2001 delivering supplies to the M/V *Edwin H. Gott* while downbound below the Soo Locks. *Jon LaFontaine photo*

Within a 20-year period beginning in 1928, several grocery vessels were constructed at the Twin Ports. The *Carroll Jean* was one of the later models, built in 1948 by Knudsen Shipbuilding at Superior. Measuring 38 feet long, the gas-powered launch was used to deliver supplies to ships visiting the port. Later renamed *Allouez Marine*, the vessel is pictured here in June 1998 at the DM&IR ore dock, moored alongside the steamer *Charles M. Beeghly* while supplies are lifted up through the engine room gangway door.

These chandler boats were common in the Twin Ports and on Lake Erie. Slightly smaller than the Knudsen hulls, the 35-foot *Tommy B.* was built at Duluth in 1931 by the Marine Iron & Shipbuilding Company. She is one of only a couple of local grocery boats that ever left the Twin Ports. She retains her original appearance in this July 2002 image at Cleveland.

The well-known mail boat *J. W. Westcott II* has made history as the only floating zip code in the U.S.: "48222." Providing 24-hour service to ships passing through the Detroit River, the *Westcott* pulls alongside while underway and mail is transferred with a pail on a rope lowered down from the ship. Sometimes crewmembers can catch or leave their ships from the mail boat as well. The *Westcott* is pictured here running upbound on the Detroit River in 2001.

Paasch Marine built the *Westcott* at Erie in 1949. It is powered by a 200-HP Detroit 6-71 diesel. Pictured here in the Detroit River tugboat race on June 23, 2001, she is battling it out with the former Army Box-L boat *Acushnet*. These two workboats do quite well in the tug race while, usually, the other smaller vessels fall back as the big tugs take the lead. The *Acushnet* is owned by Brian Williams, who is chairman of the Tug Race. After a long career with the U.S. Army, the boat was sold in 1971 into civilian hands for $3,538.18. Converted to a towing vessel, the tug spent the next 30 years working in the Northeast. Sturgeon Bay Shipbuilding & Dry Dock Company built her.

During WWII, two yards in Duluth built a series of 180-foot buoy tenders with special cut-away bows for ice breaking. The *Acacia* (WLB-406) was launched in 1944 by the Zenith Dredge Company for the U.S. Coast Guard. Laid down as the *Thistle* (WAGL-406), she was completed with her current name. This "180," as they are commonly known, is the last one in commercial service with the U.S. Coast Guard. She was built with a pair of 8-cylinder Cooper Bessemer diesels but in 1986 was repowered, along with many of her sisters, with two 8-cylinder 645 EMD diesels. These 180s all had DC electric propulsion and proved quite successful in their ice breaking abilities.

Cruising through the Duluth harbor on March 26, 1991 is the *WLB-404 Sundew*. Built during WWII at Duluth, two yards were awarded the construction contracts. The *Sundew* was built by Marine Iron & Shipbuilding, while others were built by the Zenith Dredge Company. As did most wartime government craft, these 180s had an armory in the stern, which was later removed. A single 1200-HP DC electric propulsion motor powers the Sundew. Electricity is generated by two EMD 8-645-E6 diesels. When built, she, like most, had Cooper Bessemer generators (two model GN-8 diesels). The *Sundew* was decommissioned on May 27, 2004 and donated to the City of Duluth for use as a museum vessel. She is now on display in the Minnesota Slip at Canal Park. *Jon LaFontaine photo*

The *Alder* is pictured at Marinette Marine while finishing touches are being completed on this newly constructed ship. Replacing the Sundew in 2004, the beautiful new vessel saw her first year of harsh ice conditions on Lake Superior. The vessel proved successful as an icebreaker. A tour of the vessel reveals many design similarities with the 180s that these 225-foor cutters replaced. Beginning in 1992, Marinette Marine built 16 of these cutters; *Alder* is the last of them.

The "Mighty Mac" is the godfather of all icebreakers on the Great Lakes. Built in 1944 by the Toledo Shipbuilding Company, the *Mackinaw* is powered by four 10-cylinder 38-D8-1/8 Fairbanks Morse diesels, which produce 12,000-HP. Her DC electric propulsion system performs flawlessly in the ice, just as it does with electric tugboats. The 290-foot long *Mac* is 75 feet wide and is heavily constructed with 1-5/8-inch steel ice belting on her hull. Built for the U.S. Coast Guard and originally to be named *Manitowoc*, the hull was completed with its current name and sees service all over the Lakes, although she is based in Cheboygan. In this rare image, the *Mac* is photographed breaking out the Two Harbors ore docks. It is rare for a Coast Guard cutter to go into private slips, but in this March image it is the start of navigation; it had been a couple of months since any ship had been through this ice, which is now a solid two feet thick.

During the absolute worst ice conditions when no other vessel can get through, the *Mac* can be found on the scene breaking ice and making a cut for vessel traffic to follow through. As of this writing, a replacement is being built. This new hull is also to be named *Mackinaw*, but many doubt that it will compare favorably to the 60-year veteran. She is pictured here busting out the shipping lanes across Lake Superior on her way to Duluth in March 1991. The ice is already several feet thick and even thicker where there are buildups. *Jon LaFontaine photo*

The Canadian Coast Guard's *Simcoe* is classified as a buoy tender but sees her fair share of ice breaking as well. Built in 1962 and measuring 180 x 38 x 14, this 3,000-HP diesel electric ship was constructed by the Canadian Vickers Shipyard in Montreal. For ice-breaking operations the old diesel-electric propulsion systems cannot be beat. She is pictured here on March 17, 1997 at St. Catherines, Ontario.

The *Stickleback* is part of the U.S. Geological Survey fleet in Ashland. The 41-foot patrol boat is now used as a research vessel and takes on those jobs that require shallow draft, where their *Kiyi* cannot go. She began life as the Coast Guard launch named *41379*. The *Stickleback* is powered by two V-8 Cummins diesels of 300 HP each. Stationed at Bayfield throughout the 1990s, the vessel was retired to the Duluth Coast Guard station and transferred in 2002 to the U.S. Geological Survey. She is pictured on July 22, 2003 at her home base, the Ashland ore dock.

Moored alongside the historic Soo Line ore dock downtown Ashland in July 2003 is the research vessel *Kiyi*. She is owned and operated by the U.S. Geological Survey, Great Lakes Science Center. Built in 1999, at the cost of $3.3 million, the vessel was constructed at Pensacola by the Patti Shipyard. The U.S. Army Corps of Engineers Design Center at Philadelphia designed her. The *Kiyi* has a range of 2,300 miles and is powered by a pair of Cummins KTA-19M3 diesels. She was commissioned in April 2000 and has been in service since, working all over the Great Lakes.

With sort of a "tug look," the research vessel *L. L. Smith, Jr.* is a fixture in the Twin Ports harbor, still in service with her rare Kahlenberg oil engine. Built in 1950 by and for Knudsen Brothers Shipbuilding in Superior, the 60-foot tug was used as a shipyard workboat until 1979 when it was sold to the University of Wisconsin for conversion to a research vessel. The tug has changed in appearance very little since its construction and is kept in very nice condition. It originally bore the name *H. R. Knudsen* until renamed *M. E. Kingsbury* in 1959. She was given her present name in 1979.

The research vessel *Neeskay* began life in 1953, launched by the Higgins Company at New Orleans. Higgins was instrumental in the construction of Army vessels in the 1950s, such as the 107-foot LT-class tugboats. It was originally an Army T-boat named *T-494*. The 65-footer was decommissioned in 1968 and transferred to the Mackinac College at Mackinac Island. In 1970, Peterson Builders converted the boat to a research vessel at Sturgeon Bay. At that time, she was given her present name and repowered with a 12v-71 Detroit diesel. Today, the vessel is under command of Captain Greg Stamatelakys and is based at Milwaukee, working for the University of Wisconsin.

The Environmental Protection Agency (EPA) operates several research vessels on the Great Lakes. One such vessel, the *Lake Explorer*, is based out of Duluth and began life as the Coast Guard patrol boat *82332*. During her career with the U.S. Coast Guard, she was the first vessel on the scene of the Space Shuttle *Challenger* explosion. Upon decommissioning, she was earmarked for transfer to the Venezuelan Navy, a transaction that never took place. Rebuilt as a research vessel, today she is based out of Duluth, in the EPA fleet.

The *Lake Guardian* is an EPA research vessel for the Great Lakes. She was built by Halter Marine (Hull No. 1031) in 1981 as the Off-Shore Supply Vessel (OSV) *Marsea Fourteen*. Upon the bankruptcy of Marsea Agencies Inc., the vessel's owner, she was transferred to the U.S. Department of Transportation. After a stint with the Massachusetts Maritime Academy, the *Fourteen* was reassigned to the EPA. Converted to a research vessel and strengthened to ABS ice class, the 180-foot, 850-ton vessel has a 6,000-mile range and a 79,000-gallon fuel capacity. Her propulsion is supplied by two Caterpillar D-399 diesels, producing 2,200-HP, turning 84-inch wheels set in Kort Nozzle drives. The *Guardian* can be found all over the Lakes during its season, conducting special research projects.

Pulled out at the Basic Marine shipyard in Escanaba on August 6, 2003 is the hull of the R/V *Sturgeon*. The vessel is undergoing a major reconstruction for the U.S. Geological Survey into a research vessel. Built in 1976 at Sausalito, California as the 100-foot fishing vessel *D. K.*, the boat was confiscated for running drugs and turned over to the Smithsonian Institution. Later, the vessel was in the hands of the National Biological Survey Division of the U.S. Geological Survey, based out of Cheboygan. In 2004, the vessel emerged from the shipyard with an entirely new look and has rejoined the fleet of research vessels operating on the Great Lakes from, once again, her homeport of Cheboygan.

The survey launch, *Hodge,* of the Corps of Engineers is shown here at Grand Haven on September 18, 1997. A late 2004 sale into civilian use, along with many other Corps vessels, has taken this vessel off the government roster due to budget cutbacks. The *Hodge* was built in Edmonds, Washington, in 1990 by Munson Manufacturing Company. These little twin-screw workboats were used by the Corps to take soundings and perform survey duties in various ports around the Lakes.

This "Polish Navy" craft is actually one of about 228 sisters built for the U.S. Navy. These 50-foot LCM-3 landing crafts were barely a year old when the Navy bases began converting them into yard pushboats. Sixty-seven of them were built between 1981 and 1986 on the Great Lakes at Marinette Marine. Many of the older LCM-3s and the larger 56-foot LCM-6s have since been sold into civilian service and converted to small workboats. This one, with no name other than a loving handle applied by an owner with a sense of humor, is pictured participating in the June 2003 Detroit River Tugboat Race.

Obviously photographed at Fraser Shipyards in Superior, this yard workboat was built by and for the Knudsen Brothers Shipyard in 1956. Several of these 40 to 50-foot steel tugs were built in the 1940s and 1950s by the yard for service around the port for performing shipside repairs. She is heavily outfitted with burning and welding equipment, as noted in this July 1999 photograph. Originally named *Byron S. Nelson,* the 175-HP tug was renamed in 1965 to honor shipyard foreman Wallace Kendzora.

Another shipyard repair vessel, the *Ranger II*, is based at Cleveland. As noted in this stern view from 1999, she is equipped with a welder and torch sets for handling vessel or dock repairs. Built by Hans Hansen in 1936, the workboat first entered service for George McElhaney at Toledo. Sold to G&W Ship Repair in 1950, the vessel has been stationed at Cleveland ever since.

A vessel in itself, the floating dry dock is used to lift other vessels out of the water. Smaller units are more common, but large floaters have also been built to lift massive freighters out of the water. It is essentially a barge with ballast tanks and high sides. The floating dry dock is sunk after proper blocking is set in place for the vessel they intend to lift. Once the dock is submerged, the customer's vessel is brought into position, centered in the dry dock. Once secured with lines, the onboard pumps empty the ballast tanks of the dry dock, and the unit refloats, lifting the other vessel slowly out of the water as it rests on the blocking. Heavily built, these floaters are able to lift tremendous weight using their own buoyancy. In this photo, the floating dry dock at the Basic Marine Shipyard is pictured in action with the Coast Guard cutter WTGB-101 *Katmai Bay* on the blocks. This 140-foot, 690-ton icebreaking tug has been pulled out of the water for inspection and repair.

The *Outer Island*, based at Bayfield, began life in 1942 as the landing craft *LCT-203*. Years of rumors had placed this vessel in the Normandy Invasion. The *203* definitely played her part in the war effort but the majority of these landing crafts were used to transport machinery and materials after the initial attack when temporary docks and false harbors were constructed. Built in North Tonawanda by the Bison Shipbuilding Corporation, the 115-foot LCT was sold after the war for civilian service on the Great Lakes. Today it is in use around the Apostle Islands on Lake Superior for moving machinery or specialized cargos.

On the Erie Canal, "Buoy Boats" (BB) were a once common sight. The small, numbered craft were used along the route by maintainers in the days of gas buoys and oil lamps. Today, a few remain as general workboats. Here, the *BB-152* sits behind the tug *Seneca* outside the Lyons dry dock. A Chrysler model 155 straight-6 gas engine powers her.

The Canadian work launch *Nautilass* is pictured at Whitby, Ontario on March 1, 1999. Looking a bit worse for wear, these tough little workboats are a vital part of marine contracting. Used for transporting tools, crew, and moving barges in shallow water, this powerful little craft was built in 1954 and is owned by the Canadian Dredge & Dock Company of Whitby. She measures 30 x 8 x 4 feet.

Chapter 7: BONEYARD

Eventually, all boats reach the end of their useful lives. Some go out with a bang, retiring from service and heading right to a shipbreaker who takes them apart. Others linger around for years, being sold for lighter duty or dockside use. Others are sold into private hands with grand plans of converting the vessel into something other than its original purpose. Retired vessels tend to gather in specific areas of the harbor, areas of the harbor that are out of the way and where vessels can go to die, peacefully. Most are not intentionally abandoned. The hope is that they will be used for some other purpose.

Most vessel owners have compassion for their iron and to scrap or sink a boat is a crime. The thought is, that there must be a time in the future when there will be a use for the old girl again. Into the boneyard she goes, awaiting a refit down the road. Soon the old boat becomes a source for parts. "That old tug back there has the same engine, let's go take the heads. We'll never use her again."

Vandals climb aboard, attracted to unbroken glass and collectors like the look of the brass running lights and steam whistle. Piece by piece, the old retired vessel drifts toward the point of no return. Months turn into years and her paint scheme starts to show it. Soon, the names have peeled, and her nameboards adorn the walls of an office building or a collector's basement.

Never to sail again, the old hulk is now just a candidate for scrapping. Usually found in clusters at every port, boneyards are a fascinating part of our maritime heritage. It's where old boats go to die. Boneyards can range in size from a single small fish tug pulled ashore, surrounded by other machinery such as trucks or engines, to the huge, famous, marine boneyards such as the Witte yard on Staten Island, New York.

Boneyards of fish tugs were common on the Great Lakes. As the commercial fishing industry dwindled, large fleets of old wooden tugs were pulled ashore and left to rot. Most marinas had, at one time,

In October of 2002, the *Comeaudoc* was towed to International Marine Salvage at Port Colborne, where, over the next two years, she will be dismantled. Collingwood Shipyards built her in 1960 as the steamer *Murray Bay* for Canada Steamship Lines. Her 1986 diesel repowering was the last job completed by the Collingwood Shipyard before they closed their doors. *Al Hart photo*

one end that was a storage area for old hulls whose seaworthiness was questionable. This was the place for "fixer-uppers," where dreamers pondered the feasibility of restoration of one of the old Roamers or Chris Crafts or maybe even a fish tug. With more talk than action, most boneyard residents eventually saw the excavator's claw and they were smashed down to firewood.

In the 1970s, when the Footers were constructed on the Lakes and into the iron ore recession of the 1980s, the Lakes saw dozens of old 600-foot steamers going "to the wall" for extended lay-ups, forming freighter boneyards. Just like the smaller vessels, they would fall prey to vandalism, part sources, theft, and natural erosion of their paint schemes in the harsh winters and the bright summer sun.

With today's awareness of environmental issues, boneyards have become hazards. Privacy fences do not float, so the public's only solution to hide marine boneyards is to eliminate them altogether. Waterfront development or clean-up projects usually lead to the removal of all wrecks, whether they are shipwrecks, abandonments, or retired vessels in storage. Many millions of dollars are spent each year to clean up and "beautify" our waterfront. The scars of industry are slowly healing as former commercial docks are transformed into condos, shopping centers, public parks, and recreation areas. With the removal of abandoned sites or relocation of vibrant industry, each city's waterfront property is becoming increasingly valuable. A collection of rust, oil and asbestos, floating or not, *usually* does not fit in with most waterfront development plans.

Therefore, the boneyards are cleaned out. Most vessels end up going to the local scrapyards for breaking. Often, past owners are located and forced to remove the vessel they were accused of abandoning. Other times, scrappers are hired to come in and dismantle a vessel on site. In ocean ports, steel vessels are commonly cleaned and then towed offshore for sinking as dive attractions and fish habitat on artificial reefs built by the state. Now and then, a vessel with serious historical significance is preserved by a maritime museum. In most cases, however, once a vessel is placed in a boneyard, its life is over.

In the 1980s, many steamships left the Lakes on the wires of foreign tugs, arriving at breaking yards in India, Turkey, China, Spain, and other countries that have limited environmental regulations and ship scrapping is profitable. Great numbers of ships also went to the domestic breaking yards in Duluth, Ashtabula, Thunder Bay, and at Ramey's Bend in Port

Colborne. The large boneyards of vessels were cleaned out, leaving only a handful to remain in the 1990s.

Fish tug boneyards were also destroyed, usually by heavy equipment first, followed by a little gasoline and a match. Barges and tugs in contractor's boneyards were cleaned out as well, mostly by local scrappers.

The average person walking by a boneyard can be captivated by the downcast expressions these boats seem to hold. These old iron souls often live longer than humans. Weather beaten and worn, they have persevered through trials and tribulations and many have triumphed only to forlornly await their sure deaths amongst each other. The boneyards often inspire those who want to restore the vessels as well as artists trying to express the "feelings" of the old girls. The powers that be have decided that these yards are eyesores and ruled to eradicate most, if not all, of them. So, look while you still can and remember the old boats, before they become a mere memory.

The *Comeaudoc* has seen better days than in this March 2003 photo, as workers cut past her engine room into the cargo holds. Three burners are at work, slicing through her heavy plate steel, while one section of the vessel's port side double hull is already attached to a crane, ready for removal. Large sections are set ashore, where they are processed into "prepared" steel, usually no bigger than 2 x 4-foot pieces. Alloys are separated and materials such as plastic, wood, and fabric are disposed of as trash.

The forward cabins off of the 1923 Parrish & Heimbecker vessel, *Beechglen*, rest on the carfloat *St. Clair*, equally old, in Hamilton, Ontario. On occasion, when a vessel is scrapped or converted to a barge, the pilothouse or a section of cabins are saved for other uses, such as a guest cabin, addition to a museum, or as a storage building at the dock.

The face of this classic Laker, the *L. E. Block*, wears a sad expression while rusting away in Escanaba. Built in 1927 by American Ship in Lorain, this 621-foot freighter is the last vessel to wear the logo of the Inland Steel Company. Originally containing a triple-expansion engine, she was repowered with steam turbines in 1953 and ran for her one-owner, Inland Steel, until laying up in 1981. At one time, the *L. E.* was one of the biggest ships on the Lakes. She took turns with the steamer *Harry Coulby*, breaking each other's cargo records throughout the 1930s. The vessel was purchased by an Escanaba shipyard and has been sitting at their facility since 1988.

A topic of debate around the Lakes for many years has been the fate of this old bulk carrier. Surveys have indicated her hull and machinery are in immaculate condition and the vessel could have a future working once again, if the market justifies, even if only as a barge. Even though her future is uncertain, the old *L. E. Block* has escaped the scrapers torch for the time being. This photo shows that she is still very much in use, by hundreds of pigeons that are proud to call her home.

Canada Steamship Line's handsome *Tarantau* awaits scrapping at Port Colborne in this March 16, 2000 image. Large pumps and other machinery, salvaged from ships, are in the foreground. Collingwood Shipyards built the *Tarantau* in 1965 to the typical Seaway size of 730 x 75 feet. The steam turbine powered vessel was laid up just the year before her tow for scrap, which took place on October 30, 1999. Abatement work began immediately and by autumn 2000, cutting commenced on her stern. Within one year, the vessel would be all but a memory, reduced to razor blades in the Port Colborne harbor.

Everyone seems to enjoy a good set of horns or whistles. Every vessel on the Lakes has at least one giant horn, used to produce signals for safety and operations or to salute passing ships and shoreside viewers. The *Tarantau* was one of the few ships on the Lakes endowed with a beautiful set of Leslie Tyfon steam horns, models 300 and 425. On the old lake boats, a set of twin Tyfon 300s were standard, but they don't compare with the incredible two-tone sound produced by the 300/425 combination. This same horn arrangement was used on the steamers *Edmund Fitzgerald*, *Edward L. Ryerson*, and *Lee A. Tregurtha*, to name a few. Once common everywhere on the Lakes, the sounds of the old Tyfons are slowly fading. Only a handful of steamships still carry them. When stern-mounted self-unloaders (which block the smokestacks) came into play in the 1970s, many of the ship's big steam horns were removed and replaced with modern, piston-driven air horns.

Normally hidden in the smoke stacks, these solid bronze beauties are a true work of art when viewed closely. The simple rugged design made the Tyfon a world leader in steam horns since before World War II. Many of the Victory ships, for example, were equipped with one model 300 Tyfon. Pictured here is the model 300 removed from the steamer *Tarantau* during scrapping. The horns measure about 3 feet long and weigh nearly 250 pounds. In this view of the exposed horn, you can see the electric solenoid mounted on the top, in back. This is the unit that actually "blows" the horn when the captain pulls the lever in the pilothouse. The bronze resonator is covered by the standard tin steam jacket that most Tyfons have. This jacket keeps the horn insulated and allows for better performance in freezing conditions. In today's market, a used model 300 Tyfon should bring in around $2,000.

The fading paint of a mothballed vessel reveals paint schemes of old. Here, we see Paterson Steamship Company's motor vessel *Quedoc* in long-term lay-up at Thunder Bay. On her stack, the old striping of the Hall Corporation is wearing though. The vessel began life as the *Beavercliffe Hall* and after more than a decade of sitting idle, she was sold for dismantling in 2002. She was powered by a four-pack of 12-cylinder Fairbanks-Morse 38D-8-1/8 opposed-piston diesels, each producing 2,000 HP.

Suffering a premature death, in the opinion of many people, the motor vessel *Quedoc* was only 26 years old when retired from service. This 730 x 75-foot Seaway-size bulk carrier laid up in Thunder Bay on December 20, 1991, never to sail again. Built in 1965 for the Hall Corporation, she was acquired by Paterson Steamship in 1988 and given her present name. Finally, in 2002, Jack Purvis at the Canadian Soo purchased her and her sister *Vandoc* for scrap. The vessels were towed to the North yard, near Algoma Steel, by the 4,200-HP ocean-going tug *Reliance*, also owned by Mr. Purvis. This photo, taken halfway through the process of dismantling, shows the cargo holds, keel, ballast tanks, side tanks, and the massive amount of piping from an interesting perspective. Scrapping a ship of this size and complexity is a process that can take up to several years to complete.

Abandoned on the beach of a small island at the Portage entry of the Keweenaw Waterway are three old wooden fish tugs. Abandonments like these were a common occurrence around the Lakes. Few remain intact today, because of weather, natural erosion and decay, or waterfront clean-up projects. The big tug is the *Doughboy*, built by Burger Boat for Norman Allie of Two Rivers in 1926. It was powered by a 45-54 Kahlenberg oil engine. The other tugs are the *Seagull,* on the left, and the *Rambler,* on the right. The smallest of the three, *Rambler*, was built in 1928 at Jacobsville, Michigan, and later fished by Richard Kalliainen on Lake Superior. Thanks to their sheltered position on this small island, these wrecks, which have already withstood decades of weather, will likely be around to view for many more years.

One of the first jobs the new Corps of Engineers derrick boat *H. J. Schwartz* completed was the salvage of two old fish tugs that had sunk at the dock in the Keweenaw. In 1996, these two tugs, the *Ronald E.* and the *West Bay*, were raised and placed on shore in the boneyard of the Julio Construction Company in Hancock. Pictured here, the *West Bay* sits high and dry, keeled over to port. Built in 1937 at Erie, the tug began life as the *Ruth E.* She is leaning toward fleetmate *Ronald E.*, which was also built in Erie, for the Barcelona Fish Company of Ashtabula, in 1939. Both tugs were later fished from Vermilion before coming to the Keweenaw.

Built by Harry Gamble in 1932 at Port Dover, the diesel fish tug *Almidart* was retired in the 1980s after a long career in the fishing trade. Returning to the Gamble shipyard at Dover, the tug is pictured here on March 1, 1999 resting in the boneyard, but still very much afloat, ready for her next career.

Laying on the beach at Hurkett, Ontario, in this November 21, 1998 image, is the hull of the former steam-powered fish tug *Rossport*. The 60-foot tug was built nearby at the Western Ship Building & Dry Dock Company yard at Port Arthur in 1915 as Hull No. 13. Frederick Gerow out of Rossport fished this "one owner" tug. The tug was retired around 1959 and pulled ashore. Her cabin and steam machinery had been removed for a potential rebuild that never took place.

Resting up the hill from Schooner Bay, in the woods, the hull of the old fish tug *Karin Lea* has seen better days. The 35-foot, wood-hulled tug has been over-plated with steel but was retired and pulled up in the mid-1990s. William Evanow built the tug in 1946 at Cornucopia for his own use and powered it with a 6-cylinder Chrysler Crown gas engine. Today, the hull is used as a giant fire pit outside a marina for burning brush and wooden debris.

Propped along the banks in Kewaunee, for years, was the 1928 automobile ferry *Straits of Mackinac*. Built by the Great Lakes Engineering Works at River Rouge, the 200-foot ferry was powered by a triple expansion steam engine. The vessel was retired in 1957 after the Mackinaw Bridge was constructed. Her upper works were cut away many years ago and the ferry was used as a barge and storage vessel. The ship became a pigeon coop over the years and finally, on April 10, 2003, General Marine towed the hulk out of Chicago and scuttled her 10 miles off Navy Pier in 78 feet of water as a dive attraction. Her engine room remains very much intact, with the steam engine and related machiney still in place.

Often vessels leave the Lakes and are never heard from again. Tugs, being hard to track down, are frequently "lost" by historians. In 1949, a 115-foot modern diesel tug arrived on the Great Lakes, newly constructed at New Orleans. The *S. M. Dean* was used to tow the coal barges *Maida* and *Constitution* between Toledo and Detroit for the Pringle Barge Line until 1968. It was then sold to McAllister Towing and left for the East Coast. More recently, the tug, now named *Gregg McAllister*, has been stationed at Newport News, Virginia. After many years of hard service, the powerful tug was finally sold in 2003 for scrapping. She is pictured on November 11, 2003 at Bay Bridge Enterprises in Chesapeake, Virginia, gutted and undergoing cleaning for the final states of scrapping.

Here are the "guts" of the *S. M. Dean*. The tug's machinery was removed before scrapping and resold to VonRiedel Marine Services for use in another tug. Pictured resting on the dock is the tug's main engine, an EMD 16-cylinder 567C. On the front of the engine, all the rigging can be seen, such as its governor, and water and fuel pumps. Down the side are eight test cocks, one for each cylinder, to blow the condensation out of the cylinders before starting. These same engines are used in EMD locomotives, although most marine versions are naturally aspirated whereas railroads tend to use turbochargers. To the left of the main engine in this photo, part of the tug's towing machine can be seen. Also ahead of the engine is the gearbox, which acts as a transmission for the vessel to convert the engine's power into torque at the shaft.

Resting in the woods above Thunder Bay, Ontario, is the nearly intact, 26-foot alligator tug *Hull 642* built by the Russel Brothers Company in 1946. Owned last by Garden Lake Timber of Thunder Bay, these tough little boats were used on inland lakes across Ontario and Quebec in logging operations. A heavy steel cage protects its propeller from log damage. The Russel Brothers yard at Owen Sound built the bulk of the alligator fleet in the 1940s.

The Gamble Shipyard in Port Dover has always been home to many retired workboats awaiting their fate. Dozens have escaped the scrapper's torch to live on as converted pleasure trawlers or workboats of a different sort. In this March 2003 image, moored alongside the leg of an old hydraulic dredge, is the 1937-vintage tug *J. A. Cornett*. At 65 feet long, this former Canadian Dredging Company tug has been resting in this gutted state since the 1980s. Behind the *Cornett*, the old iron tug *Jiggs* can be seen. Built by American Shipbuilding in 1911 as the fish tug *Baltimore*, she earned her fame as McQueen Marine's *Patricia McQueen* since her towing vessel conversion in 1936. Spending her last working years in Lorain, the old tug was towed to the Gamble yard and gutted sometime around 2000.

Shipyard vessels rest at the Easterly end of Fraser Shipyards at Superior in a small area that has become a boneyard for unused workboats over the past four decades. The *Todd L.*, built in 1952 as the *Robert M. Fraser*, by and for the Fraser-Nelson Shipyard, has seen virtually no service since the 1980s. In the 1970s, the tug was stationed at Two Harbors and would moor along the pier for the big steam-tug *Edna G*. One night, a few off-duty railroad workers with alcohol induced ambition, found the key, and decided to go for a joy ride. The tug ended up aground on the beach outside the harbor. The story has gotten better with age. When it is told today, the stolen tug is usually said to be the 110-foot steamer *Edna G*. Today, the old *Robert* rests on the blocks with a waterfront view, perhaps reminiscing with her fleetmate *Phil Milroy* about the good old days and her adventures at Two Harbors. The *Milroy* began life in 1957 as the Sault Ste. Marie supply boat *Merchant of St. Marys*. It was sold after just a couple of years to Fraser, who used the boat on a limited basis to lift machinery aboard the ships in port. The tug was found to be top heavy and was retired. Under the new name of *Barney B. Barstow*, the boat worked only a few years before being pulled ashore. She has not moved in several decades. Renamed *Milroy* in 1978, the tug has never seen service under that name, which has since peeled from her hull.

The pilothouse of the 80-foot tug *Traveller* sits ashore at the International Marine Salvage breaking yard at Port Colborne on April 20, 2001. Muir Brothers Dry Dock built the vessel in 1941 at Port Dalhousie, Ontario, for the C. S. Boone Dredging Company. Originally named *Dalhousie River*, the name changed to *Towmaster* after five years. In 1949, the tug was sold to Canadian Dredge & Dock and named *Shediac*; she never saw service under this name. Shortly thereafter, the boat was renamed *Traveller*. The tug was scrapped at Port Colborne in the mid-1990s. To compare size, note the pilothouse off a Ford Motor Company steamer to the right. In the background, CSL's *Tarantau* is next in line to be cut for scrap.

Partially dismantled and resting at Erie is the retired ferry *Lansdowne*. Built in 1884 by the Detroit Dry Dock Company at Wyandotte, their Hull No. 66 was a 319-foot iron steam-powered railroad car ferry. The ferry was powered by a pair of rare diagonal steam engines, which were removed from the carferry *Michigan* upon her conversion to a barge. Built in 1872, these huge Canadian engines had cylinder diameters of 50 inches and a 108-inch stroke. The vessel was converted to a railcar barge in 1970 and continued service for the Canadian National Railway. Eventually retired, the barge was sold in 1978 for conversion to a floating restaurant. Upper decks were built, one steam engine removed for scrap, and two bright orange sky top lounge sleeper cars were set upon her old ferry deck. These train cars, the *Arrow Creek* and *Gold Creek*, were both built in 1948 by Pullman Standard for the Milwaukee Road. They were sold in 1964 to the Canadian National and renamed *Mapleque* and *Trinity*, both retiring from service in 1971. The restaurant opened for business at Detroit in 1983 but closed in 1992 and the vessel was towed a few years later to Lorain for storage. Eventually, she was towed to Erie where she has since been sitting. Her next tow will likely be to the scrapyard.

Chapter 8: LIFE AFTER RETIREMENT

It is not uncommon to find old commercial vessels, or pieces of them anyway, lying around various ports on the Lakes. Well built and in fresh water, it is often only their size or propulsion that brings about retirement, long before their structural condition. Many of these hulls are fit for other uses and are given a second life after retirement.

Storage hulls are one typical use. Now and then, dock companies that store bulk cargos at indoor facilities will find themselves in need of more storage capacity. A quick solution to these short-term needs is to buy an old ship, at scrap value, and moor it at their facility. Ships coming in to offload their cargos can tie alongside the storage hull and unload directly into it. Cargos such as grain and cement can easily be stored in the clean, dry, massive cargo holds of a Laker. As the terminal needs the product, they can discharge the ship at any rate they choose.

Retired hulls have been converted into barges, either for commercial service or as platforms to build an office or shop. Retired boats, or parts of boats, often seem attractive sites for floating restaurants and many have been converted to such. The success rate for these businesses seems low. Anything that floats is a great deal of responsibility and liability for the owner. Perhaps its better to be *near* the water than *on* the water.

Old Lakeboats make good breakwalls or docks. Many old ships have been purposefully sunk as docks in places where a new facing was needed. At times when scrap rates are low, ships can be bought cheap. It was said that during the 1970s and 1980s when most of the old 500 to 600-foot classic steamships were going for scrap, they could be bought for less than $100,000 a piece. To compare, today's seaway size carriers are selling for for scrap to foreign buyers for over $1 million a piece. Several old hulls were cleaned and scuttled for use as breakwalls. In some situations, *several* ships were sunk together for construction of a breakwall. The hulls are filled with stone and scuttled, sometimes with portions of the hull left above the water, other times completely submerged.

Smaller boats, such as tugboats and fish tugs can be pulled ashore for use as display pieces or gift shops. Attempts have been made to convert some rather large tugs into pleasure craft or shoreside cottages. Viewed in an industrial setting, where everything is super-sized, these tugs appear small. However, pull a 90-foot tug out of the water and one will quickly learn that shoreside use is *very* limited. Take out a tape measure at home, lay out 90-feet by 26-feet and see how much of your backyard a harbor tug would take up.

Commercial boats under 60-feet in length tend to be more manageable and are commonly found

Where did the bow and stern go? The retired Laker *Elmglen* had her ends "chopped off" and a new bulkhead constructed in the stern. Large pumps were installed and her cargo holds were opened up into one large compartment. The finished product: a floating dry dock. These "floaters" can be easily towed between yards if needed. Blocks are set on the cargo hold floor (as with any dry dock), valves are opened, and the ballast tanks are flooded, essentially sinking the vessel. The boat to be dry-docked is towed into place and the *Elmglen* is de-watered. As air displaces the water, the unit slowly rises with enough force to actually lift its customer out of the water. She is pictured at home in Norfolk, Virginia. Renamed *R. E. Derecktor*, the conversion took place in Chesapeake in the late 1990s. Several floaters are on the Lakes as well; one has been converted from the 1907-built Laker *Elba*, which resides at Sturgeon Bay. The distinct hull lines and riveted plating of the old Lakers is still very apparent in both of these units today.

converted to pleasure craft. They are still very costly to own and operate, but there is something about a steel workboat that catches the eye of recreational boaters. They aren't fast, they aren't economical, they aren't quiet, but they are interesting to look at.

Often small boats are found to be useful in other areas of commercial work. Fish tugs have hulls similar to towing vessels and are often converted to just that. Along the same lines, towing vessels have also been converted to fish tugs. Both vessels are commonly converted for other uses, such as passenger service, research, or pilot boats. Some boats have changed their configuration to work in many different services throughout their lives.

"One person's junk is another's treasure," they say and it's true in the maritime industry as well. Old boats can be given another chance at life after retirement, but eventually, they all see the boneyards.

Resting between jobs at Baldwinsville, New York, on April 19, 2001 is the Canal Corporation's *Wards Island*. Underneath the rather plain wheelhouse and "barge-like" flat deck, one can see the unmistakable rounded hull of an old riveted steamship. Once a beautiful passenger vessel, her upper decks are long gone, as the ship was transferred from one state agency to the next for conversion to a crane boat. This simple looking boat began life with the New York State Department of Mental Hygiene as a ferry for its Manhattan State Mental Hospital. Designed by Eads Johnson, Marine Engineers, of New York in 1927, it was launched in 1929 by the New London Ship & Engine Works at Groton, Connecticut. The vessel retains many of her original quarters below deck and is powered electrically by a rare engine combination of a Cat D353 and a Cleveland 8-268A.

Here we see the old and the new. Cement boats of the La-Farge fleet are shown here at their Chicago terminal near Lake Calumet. Against the dock is the 1904 vintage steamer *J. B. Ford*, which is the last surviving vessel of the Hawgood fleet. She is also the last survivor of the "Great Storm of 1913." Initial newspaper reports during the Lakes-wide gale indicated she was among the ships missing, but the *Ford* turned up several days later, battered but still under power. The vessel is now retired and used for cement storage. Outboard of her is the brand-new cement barge *Integrity*, which was a replacement to one of their older steamers. The *Ford* is powered by a triple expansion steam engine, which last operated in November of 1985 before the vessel was laid up. After a new cement silo was constructed in South Chicago, she was towed to Superior for the same purpose in 2001. These "storage hulls" are handy to have at the facility for increased storage capacity. Several cement and grain terminals around the Lakes use old retired Lakers for storage of additional product.

Another customer for the old *J. B. Ford*, but this time it's the steamer *J. A. W. Iglehart* of 1936. Originally an Amoco tanker, this converted cement carrier is enjoying a new life of her own, after retirement. She is pictured discharging her cargo of powdered cement into the holds of the *Ford*. Moored tightly together, large hoses are connected and the cargo is transferred. The cement is pumped ashore, as needed, into trucks and used primarily in the construction trade. For some of the most historic vessels on the Lakes, this storage "gig" has extended their lives by several decades, with no end in sight.

Built in 1894 at Chicago Shipbuilding Company, the bulk carrier *Kearsarge* was retired in the early 1940s. The 328-foot steamship was dismantled at Detroit in 1948 but portions of her lived on. Sections of her plate were saved to use in construction of the small towboat *Sabadash* the following year. In addition, a good size portion of her hull from the waterline down was saved and reused in construction of a floating restaurant that still exists. "Hornblowers" in downtown Cleveland is a good place to eat, with an excellent view of the waterfront.

Interlake's *Frank Purnell* sits idle on Lake Calumet in South Chicago as a cement storage hull. Renamed *C. T. C. No. 1* by the Medusa Cement Company in 1981, the hull acts as nearly the entire cement facility: silos, pier, and all. Cement ships will raft alongside and discharge their cargos into her holds where it is stored until needed. The product can then be pumped ashore into hoppers where it is loaded into trucks. In this photo, the transfer and hopper system can be noted alongside the ship. She was originally a 1943 vintage ore carrier of the Maritimer-class.

Another Maritimer serving as a storage hull is the *Willow-glen*, laid up in Goderich, Ontario. Beginning life as Bethlehem Steel's *Lehigh*, she was sold Canadian in 1981 but retired from service after a decade in the grain trade. In this March 2003 image, she shares the harbor with the mothballed *Teakglen*, which had just been purchased to replace the aging *Willow*. Both ships, however, were offered for sale as scrap in the autumn of 2004. The *Willow* is the last Maritimer in her original configuration and was the last of the B-1 Maritimers in service with her original triple-expansion engine. She was also the last straight-decker in service on the Great Lakes with an up-and-down steam engine when she was retired in 1992.

The 1914-vintage *William H. Donner* was an ore carrier for Mahoning Steamship Company and later ran for Bethlehem Steel. This 504-foot vessel was a huge ship in her day and was powered by a 1,800-IHP triple expansion steam engine with cylinder diameters of 23-1/2, 38, and 63 inches with a stroke of 42 inches. Originally, she was built with an open bridge, something that was common on freighters of her era. In 1970, Bethlehem sold the ship to a Milwaukee firm who used her as a dockside unloading rig and storage hull. In 1992, the *Donner*, which had been converted to a crane ship in 1957, was towed up to Marinette to work in the same capacity. The crane ships were used to haul materials such as scrap and pig iron. Today, ships moor alongside the *Donner* and dockworkers use her cranes to unload their cargos. In this September 1999 image, the last of the classic crane ships is busy unloading steel ingots from the foreign vessel *Federal Oslo*.

Built by Chicago Shipbuilding, U.S. Steel's *William E. Corey* was a fleet workhorse, hauling iron ore from the mines of Northern Minnesota down the Lakes to the steel mills. She and her sisters were the largest ships on the Lakes when launched in 1905. After 50 years in service, the 558-foot *Corey* was outdated and considered too small to continue in its trade. On June 20, 1960, she was mothballed at Duluth and exactly three years later, she was sold Canadian to Upper Lakes Shipping. In order to expand their fleets, the Canadian steamship companies purchased aging American ore carriers. Renamed *Ridgetown*, the vessel soon entered the Canadian grain trade and was able to haul roughly 400,000 bushels. After only six years of operation, the vessel was retired and sold in 1970 to a marine contractor who scuttled the hull off Nanticoke for use as a temporary breakwall during construction of a new harbor. The vessel was raised in 1973 and a year later, was permanently sunk off Port Credit, Ontario for part of *their* breakwall. Serving in that capacity for more than 30 years, the vessel remains fully intact, as one can see in this 1998 photograph.

In January 1922, the Great Lakes Towing lighter *T. F. Newman* was wrecked at Conneaut and declared a total loss. A new, similar vessel was built by the Towing Company's shipyard in 1923 and also named *T. F. Newman*. "Lighters" were used to remove portions of cargo from ships to lighten their draft during groundings and other casualty situations. The second *Newman* served the Towing Company until 1949 when it was sold Canadian. Working for McLean at the Sault and later McQueen, the vessel eventually ended up at the ABM Marine dock, which is now Purvis Marine at Sault Ste. Marine, Ontario. The stripped-out hull was pulled up tight to the banks and used as a dock facing. Today, the rusted old hull of this historic vessel can still be seen, and actually driven on, as the dirt road is plowed right out onto the stern. She is pictured here on June 25, 2004. Resting on her stern is an old triple expansion steam engine from the carferry *Chief Wawatam*.

The steamer *Tampico* is pictured here beached stern first with a manmade road leading onto her decks. The 1900-vintage freighter was used as a temporary breakwall during a construction project in the 1960s at Two Rivers along with the steamer *Adrian Iselin*. Both hulls were raised after the project's completion and towed to Frankfort where they were beached about 300 feet apart from each other as new finger piers where the Luedtke Engineering Company moored their barges and tugs. Still used in that capacity, this March 1999 image reveals the *Tampico's* rounded stern, riveted hull plating, cooling water overboards, fairleads, and even traces of her former billboard lettering down the side of the hull that read "Nicholson Transit Co."

"Let 'em go!" Workers at the Algoma Steel dock at the Canadian Soo throw off the lines of a Saltie that is singling up in preparation to sail. The dock they are standing on has history greater than an order of sheet piling. It is the 600-foot hull of the steamer *Sewell Avery* built by American Shipbuilding in 1943. This Maritimer-class vessel was retired in 1981 and sunk for use as a dock facing at Sault Ste. Marie in 1987. Her smoke stack and back deck rigging were all removed immediately. In the early 1990s, her stern cabins and forward superstructure were all still in place, as was the smoke stack, sitting next to the ship, ashore. However, by the late 1990s, she had been stripped right to the main deck, her cabins and even bulwarks cut away and gravel plowed over her decks. Below the deck on which the crew is standing, may sit (submerged) the very last Lentz double compound steam engine left on the Great Lakes and, perhaps, in the world. If it is there, it definitely should be preserved in a museum but it will likely never again see the light of day.

Dozens of old Laker hulls remain around the Lakes in a form most of us would dismiss as just a pile of rocks or some old sheet piling. Often, retired Lake Carriers were an inexpensive way to build a breakwall. This selection of boulders and rusted plating is actually the complete hull of the steamer *Syracuse*, built by the Detroit Dry Dock Company in 1884 as a passenger and freight boat. The 268-foot vessel was later reconstructed into a self-unloading sand carrier and finally after 88 years of service, her 15th owner decided to scuttle her for a private breakwall in Lakeside, Ohio. Scrapped down to the main deck, the ship was dragged into place, scuttled, and filled with stone to give it the proper strength as a seawall. To the untrained eye, it looks nothing like the remains of a ship, but upon close inspection, the classic lines and riveted hull plating of a Laker are obvious.

The beautiful passenger steamer *Alabama* is spending lay-up with fleetmates *North American* and *South American* in Holland, ready for a Marshal's sale. In only a couple of years, this proud old steamer will be cut down to a barge, her engine room gutted and turned into a cargo hold. Built in 1910, the 250-foot steamship was launched by the Manitowoc Shipbuilding Company, constructed for the Goderich Transit Company of Milwaukee, who maintained ownership until 1932. *Authors collection*

What is left of the once elegant passenger steamer *Alabama* sits along the banks of the Rouge River, awaiting the scrapper's torch in this July 2002 photo. Converted to a barge in 1964, a notch had been added to her stern so a tug could push the hull. Her double bottom has given out and the leaky old hull has long since outlived her usefulness. It is important to note that most of her quarters are fully intact down below. Even on her main cargo deck, the outline of a toilet seal, shower, and drain, complete with a metal shower curtain ring that has been rusted to the deck for some 40-years, show where her washroom once was.

This elegant floating office building began life in 1928 as the Corps of Engineers hydraulic dredge *Pearl*. While her history is sketchy, the unit was built at Des Moines, Iowa, and came to be owned by the Zenith Dredge Company on Lake Superior in 1958. Working under the names *Louise, Frances Jane, Frank M. Rogall,* and lastly, *Superior*, the dredge was powered by an EMD 12-567A until her retirement in the 1980s. Zenith sold the dredge to Billington Contracting who removed its machinery and resold the hull to the owner of the Portable Products Company (inventor of the "Bucket Boss" for those of you who are familiar). Her new owner, Bob Fierek, did an incredible rebuild of the old dredge, transforming her into a truly beautiful waterfront office.

Sometimes, when a ship is scrapped, the cabins are saved for use as storage buildings or shacks around the yard. In this case, the 1907 Laker *William J. Filbert* was broken up at the Hyman-Michaels scrapyard at Duluth in 1977. Her pilothouse was removed intact and saved for re-use as a control tower for the yard's giant shear. In the background, the Norwegian ship *Goviken* takes on a load of grain. It is interesting to compare the two pilothouses. Eighty years apart in age, the *Filbert's* had been in place at the crusher eight years before the keel was even laid for the modern ocean-going *Goviken*.

A lot of sharp edges, oil, and typical tugboat dirt must first be removed if you are going to turn one into a playground! At Hamilton, the old *Bayport* has been planted in the park at its waterline and converted to the ultimate sand box toy for the kids. This historic 80-footer has kicked around between many well-known owners including Canada Steamship Lines, Foundation Maritime, Harry Gamble, and McKeil. Kingston Shipbuilding built her in 1945 for the Royal Canadian Navy as the *Banswift*. She was sold in 1947 for civilian use and given the name *Bayport* in 1962. The oversized pilothouse is not original; it came off the canal freighter *Northcliffe Hall*. Jason LaDue photo

One of the more graceful passenger vessels found on the Lakes is Georgian Bay's *Georgian Queen*, which runs out of Penetanguishene. Laid down in 1918 as the 120-foot tugboat *Victoria*, she entered service as the *Murray Stewart*. The vessel was originally powered by a triple expansion steam engine and constructed by the same yard that built the tug for its own use, Port Arthur Shipbuilding at Port Arthur, Ontario. In 1974, the old steamer was converted to a diesel passenger vessel and her cabins replaced. In this March 15, 2000 photo at its home dock, the steep sheer and heavy riveted hull plating of an old tugboat are evident.

Built by Paasch Marine at Erie in 1950, the trap net tug *Nellie III* worked out of Erie until 1962 when it was sold as a Port Authority workboat in Buffalo and renamed *Buffalo Port*. Later working as a charter fishing boat and in the 1970s named *Little Toot*, she returned to Erie, converted to a passenger boat. Undergoing yet another conversion after retirement, in 1998, the *Toot* was made into a research vessel for Ganon University. Looking better than new, and named *Environaut*, the 36-foot welded steel boat is in service at the same port where she was built, 55 years earlier.

Found in Wisconsin's Door County at the corner of Highway Q and 57, the old wooden fish tug *Amelia D.* rests in the dirt, roughly landscaped, as a simple tribute to the once thriving commercial fishing industry in that area. The 45-foot tug was once a typical gill net tug with a wooden hull that has been plated over with thin steel for reinforcement. Her main engine was a Chrysler Crown, gas powered. Not really a museum vessel or a boneyard piece, but today the *Amelia* does sit on display, slowly rotting away, acting as a reminder of the industry's rich history.

At Port Dover in March 2003, the owners of the fish tug *Alex B.* began a conversion to a pleasure craft. The 56-foot gillnet tug was built in the same port by the Gamble family in 1946 for Alexander Brown. The tug fished out of Port Dover and, later, Wheatley before returning to Dover and retiring from the fishing trade. Her cabins were removed and a new superstructure was being built at the time of this photo. Sturdy old fish tug hulls are a popular starting point for those wishing to make a retired workboat into a recreational vessel. Her old pilothouse can be noted ashore and another old tug, also undergoing a recreational conversion, is moored behind.

Since her construction in 1944, the wooden gill net tug *Nels J.* was a fixture in the small fishing village of Knife River, on the North Shore of Lake Superior. Fished by Melvin Bugge and later owned by Pete Bugge (operator of the Knife River marina), the tug was pulled ashore in the late 1980s. Everyone knew the vulnerable old black and white tug would never sail again but local affection for the old girl kept some hope alive. In 1998, her Gray Marine 6-71 diesel was sold and used to repower the bumboat *Kaner I.* A few years later, the *Nels J.* was finally sold for reuse. After a cosmetic restoration, the tug was trucked to Canal Park in Duluth and placed along the lakefront in May 2001 to be opened as a snack shop. The tug is pictured later that year, with her front row seat at a November gale. Open during the summer months, the fish tug is now a place to stop and have lunch and, of course, fish is on the menu. Behind the tug is the pilothouse from a retired Laker, now converted into a gift shop.

Chapter 9: MUSEUM VESSELS

The Great Lakes are rich in history and the surrounding residents care about preserving their heritage. Most of the towns along the shores were built because of maritime industry. Whether it was commercial fishing, pulpwood, or iron ore, these towns grew in an era of plentiful industry jobs and a booming economy. The cities and small towns along the Lakes adjusted to the downfall of these industries but they are proud of their roots and honor this heritage with local marine museums or displays in the parks.

Each lake has a specific scenic route around the lake marked with signs called a "Circle Tour." Circle Tours are popular vacations for many people, including locals, and give an up-close look at the beauty of the shorelines and towns along the way. A Tour on any of the Lakes will include lighthouses, parks with anchors and other industry items, marine and industry museums, abandoned docks or shipwrecks and, of course, the museum vessels.

As towns recover from the scars of abandoned industry, their waterfront development plans often include maritime parks or museums that have commercial dock space still available. Boats with

historical significance, from freighters to small workboats, are often preserved in these settings and are opened for tours to the public.

Many small fishing villages proudly display old fish tugs as their mascots. Historical foundations often own museum vessels and can market them as traveling showpieces. Their restorations are extremely accurate—no detail is overlooked. These restorations take the vessel back in time and freeze it in the era it once worked.

Other vessels are owned by the cities in which they are displayed. They sit peacefully in park-like settings but many do not stand the test of time because their restorations are simply cosmetic. Fish tugs, for example, will not last forever, sitting outdoors, exposed to the elements. These casual display pieces are generally removed and discarded when they are beyond repair but their time spent on display does not go to waste. They provide years, if not decades, of public viewing. They give people a chance to document design and photograph the vessels' lines. When one of these pieces is eventually destroyed, its legacy lives on in art and in museum files.

Under command of Captain John Wellington, the 1919-vintage U.S. Shipping Board tug *John Purves* performs her last big towing job, with the steamship *J. L. Mauthe* in tow. On New Year's Eve 1996, the tow makes their final turn, leaving the Duluth harbor, bound for Sturgeon Bay, where the *Mauthe* will undergo a conversion to a barge. The *Purves* was built as the steamer *Butterfield* by Bethlehem Shipbuilding at Elizabeth, New Jersey, based on the plans of a standard 150-foot design. Her triple expansion steam engine was replaced in 1957 when she was converted to twin screw and repowered with two EMD 12-567A diesels taken from the LST-1006 (which had been converted to a barge). Shortly after the *Mauthe* tow, the *Purves* was put into reserve status. In 2003, she was finally donated to the Door County Maritime Museum at Sturgeon Bay, where a restoration is underway.

In this April 1997 photo, the museum ore carrier *William A. Irvin* stands proud at the Port of Duluth in the Minnesota Slip, just inside the canal entrance. The famed aerial lift bridge can be seen in the background. Built in 1938, this beautiful Laker served U.S. Steel in the ore trade for 40 years before being laid up on December 16, 1978. She and her sisters were the first class of vessels powered by direct-geared turbines and the first to have watertube boilers. Joining the large flotilla of retiring 600-foot steamers, the *Irvin* sat around for several years, watching tugs come for her fleetmates, one at a time, to haul them off to the shipbreakers. Still sitting in reserve in 1986, the vessel was sold to the City of Duluth and restored for museum use. Towed by the tugs *Dakota* and *Sioux* to her current berth, the *Irvin* has become a landmark in the Duluth harbor and a popular tourist attraction in the summer. Her beautiful interior and extensive tour is well worth the time.

Other boats are victims of poor planning. Preserving a vessel as a museum piece is not easy. Iron is not meant to float. Only through careful design are thousands of tons of steel made to float on water. If such a vessel is not properly maintained, the fact is, it *will* sink. The Great Lakes are subjected to harsh weather conditions with especially brutal winters, which take a great toll on vessels. Water left in pipes will freeze and as the ice expands, steel pipes crack and couplings and valves burst. When spring thaw comes, boats sink. Museums often do not have the funding or resources to dewater a vessel and to hire divers, salvage equipment, and cranes. Another big concern is that all boats contain fuel and lubricants. Any object containing oil is a potentially huge liability.

Vessels left in the hands of the inexperienced or groups without enough funding are in danger of destruction, either by human error or natural causes. Many attempts to save commercial vessels have failed and the boats were eventually sunk or dismantled. For those who care, it is heart breaking to see a restoration fail after much effort and funding has been exhausted in an attempt to save a boat. At that point, the common feeling is, "She was better off left in the boneyard."

Preserving a boat for static display is difficult enough. Some organizations attempt to restore vessels to fully operating condition. With great credit to these groups, several have been successful. A functioning museum vessel gives a unique opportunity to show how it once was. Steam power, direct reversing engines, wooden-hull fish tugs, and single screw tug-

boats are all becoming things of the past. Even just one of these vessels preserved in working condition allows future generations to see the equipment that built and supported these towns.

Several particularly important pieces have been saved around the Great Lakes. On Lake Ontario, the former Army tug *Nash* is on display in Oswego. She is kept in operational condition and is used several times throughout the season. An old Erie Canal Derrick boat and the fish tug *Eleanor D.* (1946) are also on display. Lake Superior is home to two additional former Army LT-class tugs, both sister ships to the *Nash*. The *Ludington* is on display in Kewaunee and the *Lake Superior* is on display at Duluth.

Buoy boats can be found all along the Erie Canal. Some are showpieces to the entrance of the Canal Corporation's maintenance facilities or displayed in public places. At Kingston, New York, two excellent museums can be found; one has the former Canadian McAllister tug *Mathilda,* and the other has the canal tugs *Frances Turecamo* and *Chancellor*.

On Lake Erie, Buffalo is home to several Navy ships including the destroyer USS *The Sullivans*, submarine USS *Croaker,* and cruiser USS *Little Rock*. In Cleveland, the Cleveland-Cliffs Laker *William G. Mather* can be found, along with the submarine USS *Cod*. Another Cliffs steamer, the *Willis B. Boyer*, is on display at Toledo. It is well worth a tour. Another Laker from that era, the steamer *Valley Camp* is a floating museum at Sault Ste. Marie, Michigan; her holds are used to display artifacts. In Detroit, the Bob-Lo steamers *Columbia* (1902) and *Ste. Claire*

Resting on the beach at Little Sand Bay on Lake Superior is the fish tug *Twilite*. Built in 1937 by Halvor Reiten at Bayfield, the tug was fished by the Hokenson family at Little Sand Bay until 1953. In 1982, the Park Service rebuilt the site, including the old fish tug. The *Twilite* was restored to its original configuration, including returning the original Caterpillar tractor engine that powered her in 1937. The 34-foot wooden tug is a remarkable example of a once-common design of Lake Superior fish tugs. About ten minutes off Highway 13, west of Red Cliff, at Little Sand Bay, the Hokenson Fishery site is well worth a visit for those who enjoy the history of commercial fishing on the Lakes.

(1910) may have bright futures as museum vessels. In 2004, the *Ste. Claire* was moved to Lorain, where a restoration was begun by a couple of ambitious entrepreneurs with a heart for history.

The buoy tender *Bramble* is kept on display, in fully operational condition, at Port Huron, where the St. Clair River meets Lake Huron. Port Huron also has the 1920 vintage lightship *Huron*, which was decommissioned in 1970. It was one of the earlier restoration efforts on the Lakes.

Beating them by a couple years, the Peterson family was inspired in 1967, to purchase the 1907 passenger ship *Keewatin* for museum purposes. The beautiful 346-foot steamer was moved into the tiny recreational harbor of Douglas, Michigan, and has been open for tours each summer ever since. In 1969, the vintage steam G-tug *Reiss* joined the *Keewatin* and spent 35 years alongside her until she was donated in 2004 to a Duluth-based preservation group.

Chicago is home to a German U-boat. The Museum of Science and Industry holds the *U-505*, a 252-foot long submarine captured on June 4, 1944 in the Atlantic Ocean. The Wisconsin coast of Lake Michigan is a scenic drive and its small port towns include lighthouses and fish tugs. Door County is home to many fish tugs along with a fantastic museum that has the 150-foot tugboat *John Purves* on display in Sturgeon Bay. In Manitowoc, the Gato-class submarine USS *Cobia* is open for tours as part of the beautiful Wisconsin Maritime Museum. The museum also has a functional steam engine with an electronic chadburn that can be operated by any museum visitor. This triple expansion steam engine came out of the famed carferry *Chief Wawatam*, which was reduced to a barge at the Soo.

Across the lake in Muskegon is another submarine. The USS *Silversides* can be toured along with the 1927 cutter *WMEC-146 McLane*. Muskegon is also home to the 361-foot passenger ship *Milwaukee Clipper*, which last operated in 1970 as a Lake Michigan ferry. Attempts to bring her to Milwaukee or Duluth as a museum failed and she was finally moved to Muskegon in 1998. Up river from her, the *LST-393* is on display. The *393*, a WWII U.S. Navy landing ship, was converted to a Lake Michigan carferry. The vessel last operated in 1973 and was recently sold for museum use.

Lake Superior is home to several museum vessels, including the well-known steam tug *Edna G.* at Two Harbors and the U.S. Steel straight-decker *William A. Irvin* at Duluth. The buoy tender *Sundew* is also open for tours at Duluth. She was built locally 60 years before her retirement. Along the Duluth Ship Canal, the local marine museum is a popular attraction. Outside the doors, you will find the 45-foot U.S. Army ST-class tug *Bayfield*, which last worked for the U.S. Army Corps of Engineers.

Based in Duluth, the Northeastern Maritime Historical Foundation has accumulated the largest collection of historical tugboats in North America. The 1908 *Mount McKay* and 1896 *Islay* are both in the museum fleet, powered by some rare Kahlenberg engines. The steam tugs *Q. A. Gillmore* and *Spirit of Algoma* are owned by the foundation, as is the 1929 vintage fish tug *Jane*.

In Bayfield, the fish tugs *Ruth* and *Dawn* are on display, along with the original pilothouse off the carferry that is now known as the *Viking I*.

Museum vessels are often taken for granted. The intense labor and funding dedicated to these projects should not be overlooked. Maintaining a commercial vessel is not an easy task and the museums and cities around the Lakes who have undertaken these projects deserve great credit. They are definitely the highlight of any Circle Tour.

Who could not recognize the graceful lines of the steamer *Edna G.*, built in 1896 for the Duluth Missabe & Iron Range Railway? Spending her entire career based out of Two Harbors, on the North Shore of Lake Superior, the tug remains there today as a mascot for the town. *Edna* retired in 1981 as the last steam powered tug in commercial service on the Great Lakes. The 110-foot riveted tug is powered by a fore and aft compound steam engine with cylinder diameters of 18 and 40 inches and a bore of 30 inches. The 700-HP tug was, and still is, one of the most powerful steam tugs found on the Great Lakes. She rests at the same mooring from which she always worked, next to the DM&IR ore docks in Two Harbors and is opened for tours during the summer months.

Inbound for the Duluth piers on September 21, 2002 is the 1908-vintage tug *Mount McKay*, owned by the Northeastern Maritime Historical Foundation. Originally named the *Walter F. Mattick*, the 80-foot riveted iron tug was built by Benjamin Cowles at Buffalo and owned by the builder himself in a partnership with the vessel's namesake, Walter F. Mattick. Sold to the Corps of Engineers in 1924, the tug was renamed *Marinette* and served at Milwaukee until 1947 when the tug was sold Canadian. She worked in the rafting trade on Lake Superior for many years, owned by Great Lakes Paper as the *Esther S.* Given her present name by the J. P. Porter Company in 1966, the tug was last employed commercially by Jack Purvis at the Canadian Soo, who retired the vessel in 1989. Her original H. G. Trout Company fore and aft compound steam engine was replaced, after her transition to Canadian flag, with a giant C-6 Kahlenberg oil engine that still powers her today.

Pictured outbound in the Genesee River, bound for Lake Ontario, the tug *Nash* departs Rochester on a warm August 2000 day. Jakobson built the 114-foot LT-class tug in 1943 at Oyster Bay, New York, for the Transportation Corps as the *Major Elisha K. Henson*. After decommissioning in 1947, it was transferred to the Corps of Engineers where it enjoyed a 44-year career before acquisition by the H. Lee White Marine Museum at Oswego. The tug remains on display at Oswego and is kept in a beautiful, operational condition. *Jason LaDue photo*

The graceful passenger steamer *Keewatin* rests in shallow water at a Douglas marine museum. Mr. R. J. Peterson, who had the foresight to purchase this luxurious Great Lakes vessel from the scrappers in 1967, owns her. Squeezing it into the small marina community must have been an amazing feat and the Petersons have done a superb job in maintaining her ever since. Her wooden decks, tall stack, beautiful staterooms, and interior are well worth a tour during the summer months on Lake Michigan.

Built in 1907 at Glasgow by the Fairfield Company, the *Keewatin* was launched just a few miles upriver from the *Lusitania*, built the same year at John Brown's yard. Upon reaching Montreal, *Keewatin* was cut in half to transit the St. Lawrence and Welland Canal locks. The Canadian Pacific Railway operated her until her retirement in the 1960s. She was sold for scrap in 1966 but purchased for museum use within months. The vessel was saved almost entirely intact and has since been a proud display, representing a once common fleet of passenger ships on the Lakes. On board, her brass and woodwork shine in this pilothouse view from 2004.

Lying "on the hip" of the passenger steamer *Keewatin* in Douglas in this 1997 photo is the tug *Rolland E. Peterson*. Built in 1913 by and for the Great Lakes Towing Company, this 84-foot steamer is the last remaining original configuration "G-tug" in the world. This famous class of tugs was, and still are, the primary tugs used for ship assistance and ice breaking in every major U.S. port on the Lakes. Originally named *Q. A. Gillmore*, the tug was declared surplus in 1931 and sold to the C. Reiss Coal Company. In 1933 she was renamed *Reiss*. When built, her Hodge machinery was salvaged from an older tug scrapped the same year. To this day, her original 1880's steam engine and coal-fired boiler remain in place. Retired in 1968 and sold to Roland J. Peterson for museum use at Douglas, the tug has been a mainstay in the small harbor for more than 30 years. Donated in 2004 to the Northeastern Maritime Historical Foundation, the tug was dredged from its shallow water berth in preparation for a tow to a shipyard for a long overdue dry-docking.

The USS *Silversides* (SS-236), a Gato-Class electric submarine, is on display and open for tours at Muskegon. Built for the U.S. Navy in 1942 at Vallejo, California, she is powered by four opposed-piston Fairbanks-Morse diesels of 1,800 HP each, producing electricity for a 5,400-HP DC electric propulsion system. The sub was decommissioned in 1946 and brought to the Chicago area for use as a training vessel for the U.S. Navy. It has been a museum vessel in Muskegon since 1987. Several other interesting museum submarines exist on the Lakes, including the *Cobia* at Manitowoc, the *Croaker* at Buffalo, the *Cod* at Cleveland, and the German U-boat *U-505* ashore at Chciago. The Great Lakes shipyards produced many submarines for the U.S. Navy, but few remain today.

The decommissioned Coast Guard buoy tender *WAGL-234 Maple* rests at Cheboygan. Sold for museum use in 1994, the boat was built in 1939 by Marine Iron & Shipbuilding in Duluth for the Coast Guard. She was transferred to the EPA in 1973 and converted to a research vessel. Named *Roger R. Simons*, the boat worked until 1991 when it was transferred to the General Services Administration for disposition. The boat was laid up in Milwaukee during that time. The 122-foot steel vessel was powered by twin National Superior diesels until her repowering with a 4-pack of Detroit 6-71s. Her future as a museum vessel is questionable, as it was offered for sale in one of the later 2004 *Boats & Harbors* publications.

Built in 1896, the *Meteor* is the last whaleback in existence, above the water. These uniquely designed bulk freighters were built by Alexander McDougall at American Steel Barge Company in Superior. Launched as the *Frank Rockefeller* and owned by McDougall, the ship was later converted to carry automobiles and finally reconstructed into a tanker in 1943. This final conversion allowed this particular ship to last as long as it did. Finally retired in 1969, it was sold for museum use four years later and towed to Superior where it has been land locked at Barkers Island and open for tours ever since. Many tend to take this incredible piece of history for granted since it has been a museum for as long as most of us can remember. For any history buff traveling around Lake Superior, a tour of the *Meteor* is a must.

Photographed landlocked and on display at a Barkers Island park in Superior are the steam dipper dredge, *Col. D. D. Gaillard* and the 36-foot wooden Coast Guard rescue launch *36522*. The *Gaillard* was built by the Hartman-Greiling Company of Green Bay in 1916 and, although based in Duluth, served all over the Great Lakes, taking on some of the heaviest dredging projects ever. Her massive steam boiler, main hoist engine, and numerous auxiliary donkey engines made this a living, breathing, creature when she was at work, tearing into the rocky river bottoms with her gigantic bucket and sharp teeth (the sight of steam and noises are indescribable to those who could not witness it for themselves). She was decommissioned in the early 1980s and donated to the City of Superior for display next to the Whaleback ship *Meteor*. Over the years, the vulnerable wooden upper superstructure of the *Gaillard* fell victim to neglect and vandalism. In 2001, the decision was made to scrap her.

Billington Contracting was awarded the contract to dismantle the vessel where it sat but instead, a strategic salvage plan was formed to dig the vessel out of the landlocked berth where she had been for almost 20 years. Many had serious doubts about the condition of her hull after sitting in the moist ground for that length of time. A dike was built around the dredge and water was pumped in; the vessel was refloated in its own little pond. Since the lake level was several feet lower than when the dredge went into the park, she had to be let down slowly, almost like transiting a lock. The tug *Seneca* was on hand to start pulling when the dike was quickly opened. The *Gaillard* quickly set sail, once again, in the Twin Ports Harbor. To everyone's amazement, her hull was in immaculate condition, right down to the painted draft marks. Her confident owner, Bob Billington, had completed his share of creative salvage jobs over the years and with the removal of the *Gaillard*, he ended up with one beautiful spud barge. Her ladder had to be cut off and scrapped to lighten the hull before removal. Although this historic museum piece came to a tragic end, after retirement, it did last another twenty years in the park, perhaps enough to teach one more generation what the big steam dippers were all about.

The Coast Guard motor lifeboat *36522* sits ashore, on display, at Barker's Island in August 2002. These 36-foot Coast Guard boats were built in the shipyard at Curtis Bay, Maryland. The wooden boat was offered "free to a good home" the same year that reconstruction plans were introduced for the museum area at Barker's. The *36522* left town on November 19, 2004, bound for Virginia's Barrier Islands Center, on the eastern shore, for display. If a new owner had not come forward, the old lifeboat may have been destroyed.

The steamer *Derrick Boat No. 8* sits landlocked at Oswego. Built in 1925, the crane barge worked on the Erie Canal for 60 years. Her spuds, winches, and main hoist were all operated by steam generated by an Ames Ironworks boiler. The riveted steel vessel had wooden fendering and superstructure that are still in place today. The main stick is mounted on a turret that can swing 180 degrees. She is capable of lifting 150 tons, almost 3/4 of the vessel's own weight. In 1984, the barge was donated to the H. Lee White Museum at Oswego.

Laying in the 104th Street slip on the Calumet River in this 1996 image is the laid-up steamship *Milwaukee Clipper*. Losing its mooring to a new casino ship, the *Clipper* had been recently moved from Hammond, Indiana. Built as the *Juniata* in 1905 by American Shipbuilding, the beautiful passenger steamer was reconstructed into an automobile ferry in 1941 and given its current name. The vessel laid up in 1970 and served as a clubhouse and restaurant around the Chicago area before entering retirement. In 1998, the vessel was towed by Andrie Inc. to Muskegon and made into a museum. The vessel has since received a new coat of paint in the same scheme that she wore while in operation.

If you visit Muskegon, this rusted old automobile ferry will not be recognized. Today, she wears her military colors and is open for tours as a museum vessel. Restored to her former glory and renamed *LST-393*, this former U.S. Navy landing craft was built in 1942 by Newport News Shipbuilding. The 328-foot vessel participated in the Normandy Invasion and was awarded three battle stars for service. Decommissioned in 1946, she was converted into an auto carrier and renamed *Highway 16* in 1948. The vessel had operated on Lake Michigan since that conversion until her retirement in 1973. She is pictured at Muskegon in March of 1999.

The *Buddy O.* is the old wooden fish tug on display outside the local museum in Two Rivers. Built by Sturgeon Bay Boat Works in 1935, the 36-foot tug fished out of Frankfort and South Haven before coming to Two Rivers in 1946 to finish out its long life. Because the operator's visibility is severely limited, the classic old gill net tug had its stern pilothouse raised. It appears that *Buddy* did not escape the shingle and tar roofing so common on these tugs.

Ugh The Tug sits ashore in an uncertain state at Kenosha on June 25, 1999. Built by the Geary Boiler Works at Ashtabula, she has gained her fame as the first electrically welded commercial vessel on the Great Lakes. It is said that her keel was initially riveted and that the crew was convinced to finish the project by welding. Originally named *Dorothea M. Geary*, she served as a workboat for the Geary Company, a leader in ship repairs during their day. She was later stationed at Chicago, working for the Independent Boiler & Tank Company, but upon retirement, was donated to the Sea Scouts and renamed *Ugh The Tug*. In 2004, the vessel was donated to the Ashtabula Marine Museum, a fitting place for the old girl to go on display. Launched in July 1915, the vessel today shows little of her original appearance beyond that famous experimental hull.

Sitting in the back basin of the Philadelphia Naval Yard on October 28, 2003 is the heavy cruiser CA-134 USS *Des Moines*. Waiting in line to be scrapped, the vessels that once surrounded her are now all gone, falling prey to the scrapper's torch in the near-by dry docks. In the 1980s, a campaign began to bring sister ship CA-148 USS *Newport News* to Duluth as a museum vessel and veterans' memorial. After the deadline for that vessel passed and she was sent away for scrap, focus shifted to the *Des Moines*. Finally, in 1998, the controversial topic was put to a public vote and the idea of using tax dollars to relocate and restore the ship was rejected. Many thought the idea of a warship with no Great Lakes connection was a waste of money. Others protested the idea

of a warship in general, even though the *Des Moines'* career was reasonably peaceful. The sister ship CA-139 *USS Salem* is a museum vessel in Quincy, Massachusetts. Bethlehem Steel built both of the 716-foot cruisers at Quincy; their keels were laid in the spring of 1945 and construction was finished nearly four years later. Built as the heaviest cruisers in the world, the three sisters were the first vessels to have completely automatic rapid-fire 8-inch guns. Weighing in at 17,000 tons, the *Des Moines* is powered by a set of steam turbine engines that produce an incredible 122,000-SHP. She has eight Babcock & Wilcox boilers and will hold 2,600 tons of bunker fuel. It is only a matter of time before the old girl feels water rushing against her bow for the last time, as she goes to the graving docks for dismantling.

More than any other museum vessel, this close-up of the wooden-hulled schooner *Alvin Clark* gives us a look back into our past. The *Clark* was a merchant ship built in 1846 at Trenton, Michigan. Foundering in Green Bay on June 29, 1864, the vessel was caught in an awful gale and lost along with three of her five crewmembers. Diver Frank Hoffman, who had been hired to free a commercial fisherman's nets that were caught on an obstruction, accidentally discovered the wreck in 1967. That obstruction turned out to be the schooner *Alvin Clark*. Hoffman found the schooner to be in amazing condition, well preserved thanks in part to the chilly waters of Lake Michigan. The star of an amazing salvage story, the *Clark* was brought to the surface in 1969. The 113-foot, three-masted schooner had not seen the light of day for more than 100 years. Placed on display in Menominee, as this image shows, the ship that was found well preserved at the bottom of the bay began to decay once removed from the water. After it was raised, the owner did not have the funding to properly maintain the vessel. Other groups were solicited to take on the restoration, but none were found. The poor old schooner that was given a second chance at life was finally laid to rest by a bulldozer in the mid-1990s. One of the most serious tragedies in maritime preservation, the loss of the *Alvin Clark* should be a lesson to us all: some vessels are best left alone. *Jon LaFontaine photo*

More Great Titles From Iconografix

All Iconografix books are available from direct mail specialty book dealers and bookstores worldwide, or can be ordered from the publisher.
For book trade and distribution information or to add your name to our mailing list and receive a **FREE CATALOG** contact:

Iconografix, Inc. PO Box 446, Dept BK Hudson, WI, 54016
Telephone: (715) 381-9755, (800) 289-3504 (USA), Fax: (715) 381-9756 info@iconografixinc.com

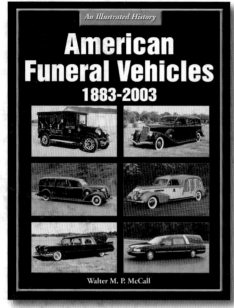
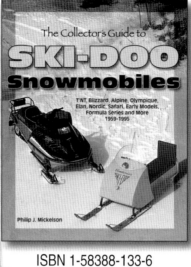
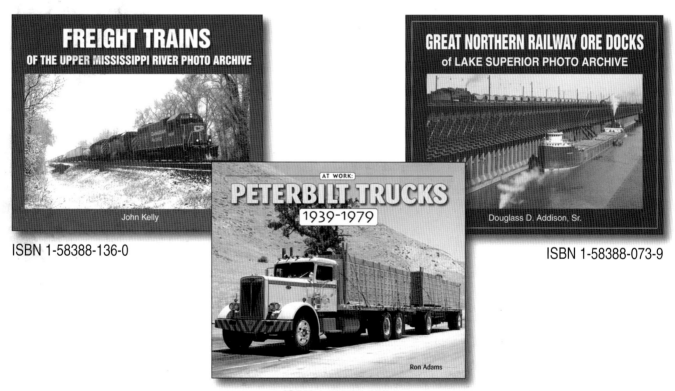